THE SICILY PAPERS

MICHELLE
ORANGE

First Edition, 2006

© 2006 Michelle Orange

All rights reserved.

ISBN 13: 978-0-9749541-4-1
ISBN 10: 0-9749541-4-4

Library of Congress Control Number:
2006930096

Short Flight / Long Drive Books
PO Box 1658
Ann Arbor, MI 48103
www.hobartpulp.com/minibooks

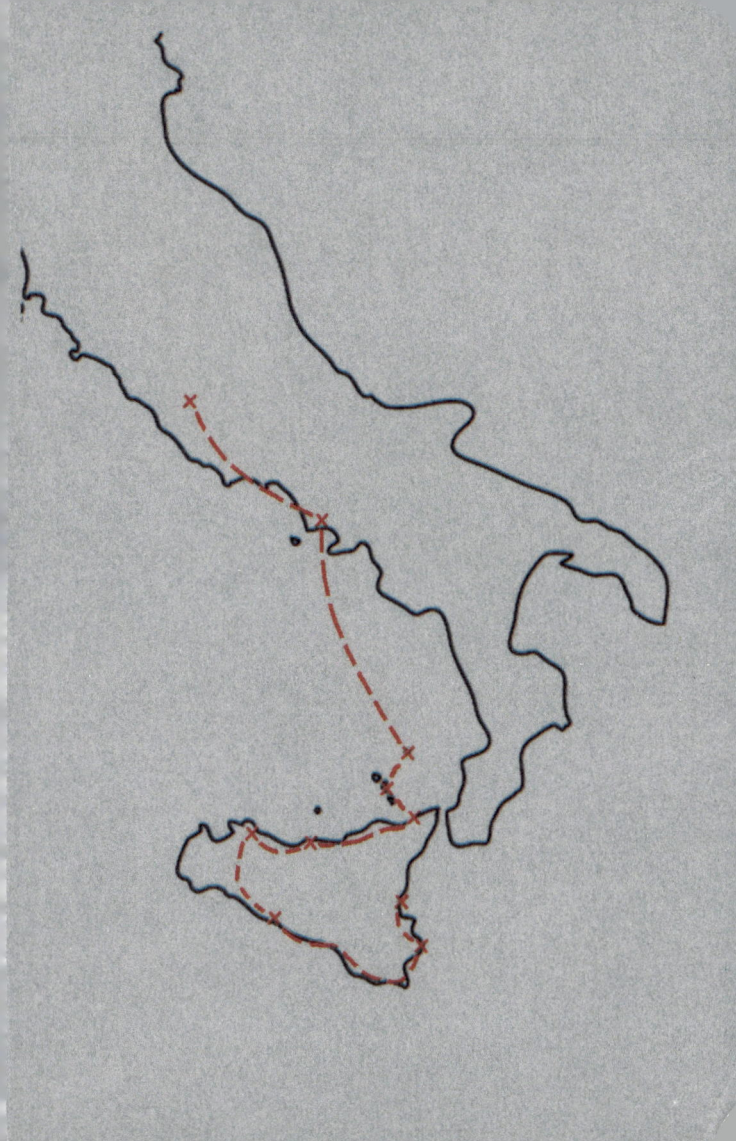

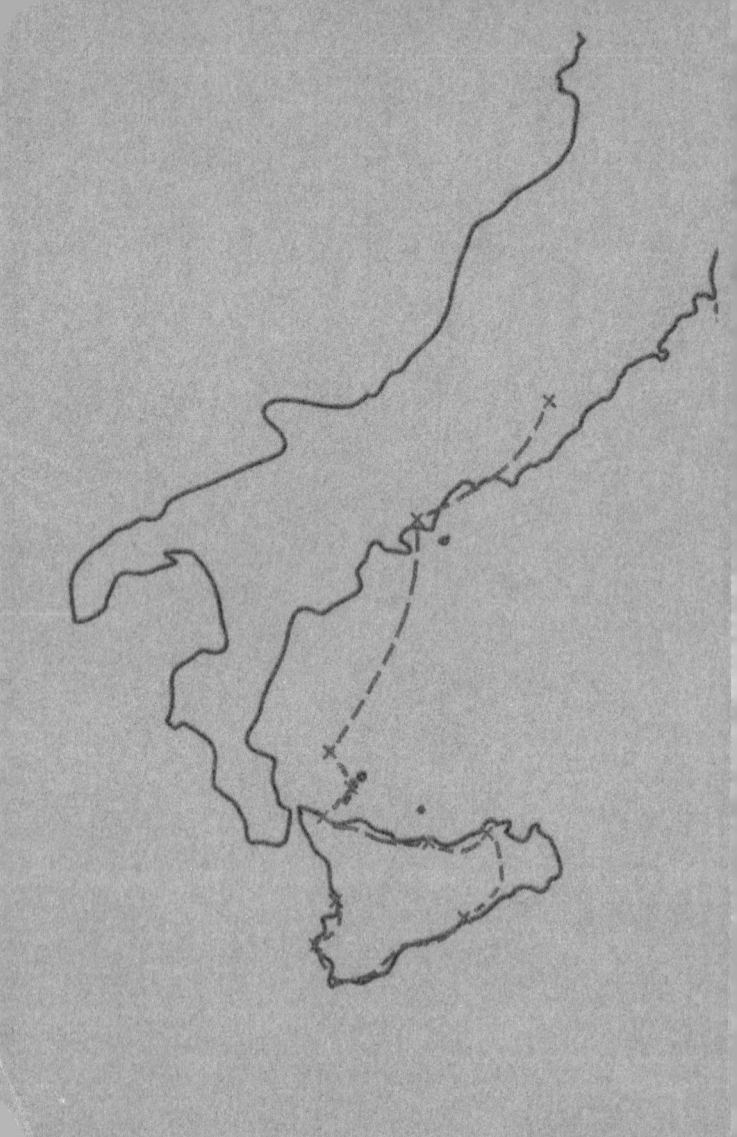

*Who is left
that writes these days?
But you and me
we'll be different.*

"The Letter", PJ Harvey

April 19, 2003

Dear B,

I am on the plane now, after the usual ordeal. I wonder if you are thinking that I am about to go. Because I am! So many children in the airport today. And I mean little babies. I always wonder, why do they make such young kids fly? It must be horrible for them. But B, guess what? I got a really great seat, and so far—no one beside me! I'm in heaven. I think I may have just jinxed myself. Oh well. Here they are. Two boys. Kind of cute. Two buddies. Wonder where they are going. I think they are going to annoy me. Oh wait, they're annoying me already. He's talking about all the money they raised for their business. He's going to Africa. Ghana. His buddy is going to

Sweden. Oh God, now it's about the girls. They're so hott!!! Way hotter than Toronto girls. OK I officially want to die. Dudes from Queens University suck. These guys sound like they're Yankees. Jesus. I get enough of that at home. Who gives a shit if you took politics and economics? Is this what John sounds like when he talks? I really want one of those water bottles they have in first class. I'm totally going to steal one. I can see that from here.

So what are you up to? Have you cried yet? Like I mentioned, I think you will recover swiftly and absolutely. Oh my God I hate these guys. They can't stop talking about school. They just called one of their female professors a bitch. Ooh, Swedish girls, they're so hot. Fuck a duck. "All the girls like taking her courses cause she definitely favours girls." This guy's just saying that cause she accused him of plagiarism. She was probably right too. They call normal girls "chicks". I looooove that. Why don't you just board this plane and shoot me right between the eyes? Buddy went to the London School of Economics. He loved London by the way. Took political theory. London is "a sweet town." How did this guy who sounds like such an asshole manage to accomplish so much? He just mentioned how he's going to look up some "local hotties" during his layover in Frankfurt. If he says "sweet" one more time I'm gonna die. I remember on my flight home from France last year I was bumped up to 1st class and I was scamming the flight attendants for more fruit. It was Air France, they were speaking French and I heard the man say to the woman that I was quite the little coquette. Also, when I left work I said goodbye to Carol and as I was going I heard her turn to the person beside her and say "She's our best export!" That made me really happy. She has seen me go to Europe every year since I started. She's a nice girl. Woman, I should say, she's got to be well over 40.

So that happened. I gave up writing on that flight fairly early on. What knobs those guys were. I had to learn about the relative hotness of every nationality of women in the world. Now I know how Beavis and Butthead would be with graduate degrees. Flight went by OK except for them. Now I am in the Munich airport waiting for my flight following a ridiculous 30 minute flight from Frankfurt. I barely had time to pound back a dwarf-sized diet coke before we were back on the ground again. No doubt you are sleeping soundly at this moment, post-White Stripes and are dreaming pleasant dreams about Meg W. I am seated, like a

I started counting the # of times he said "sweet"

good little neurotic, right in front of the departures listings. Nah, I'm not so neurotic, I was just passed out for about an hour upstairs and woke up to a mom reading a story to her kid. I was interested for a while but it didn't last so I went for a walk. There is a flight listing here for Philadelphia, it leaves at 12:15. I've always liked the name "Stuttgart", it's so much fun to say. So tell me, in your head, what were the movies you guessed for the plane? Were they Harry Potter + The Hurricane?

As annoying as the boys on the plane were, I still had to fight the urge to rest my head against the one's shoulder. In my dream I remember that you had glasses and I remember that you drew me very close and held me very tight. It's true! It's gay but true. I remember also that it felt so good, like clean sheets tucked in by a very industrious hand. I think we were on the floor and I folded my legs over yours. It's a convoluted-sounding posture but actually very comfortable.
-oh wait- my new gate is A10—good thing I'm paying attention. I feel half dead and look about ¾'s. Funny about this airport, people are smoking <u>everywhere</u>. I've never been to Germany before. I feel a little funny about it. Can I use funny in a sentence again? Funny!

On the way to the airport in my mom's convertible she asked me if I would be meeting anybody else in Sicily and I *sighed* and said "I doubt it."
"The trains must run on time!!"
Germans.

They apologize so much when they announce delays. I hear real shame in their voices. Maybe I should see if I can post this to you here. Do I have time? Do I have envelopes? I am starting to get calm, the closer I get to Italy. I have to say, I was in a bad state leading up to this trip. I don't know how it happens. I am astounded. After I got home last year, I felt changed, I felt much stronger. How do things slide back to the shameful way they were? I wonder about people's lives. Like those guys on the plane. What's going on there? They were such convincing caricatures, but in a way their talk made me feel small, all the big talk about careers and girls and partying. I think I said this already but I have a deep envy for people who speed skate through their 20's, taking the turns with especial ease. Bastards.

Well I should stop writing on that note or things are going to get maudlin. Why can't I live in Italy all the time? I'd be a better person. My dad didn't recognize me when I showed up in Florence last year. I hate that life is like this. I really hate myself sometimes.

---

this thing ran out of propane after about an hour. What will I do tonight? Come over!

Hi Kid. Finally I am in Siracusa in maybe the cutest apartment in the world. It's such a shame, in a way, that I have it all to myself. Also I have just positioned the gas-powered space heater about a foot from where I am sitting, because for some reason it is about 10 degrees colder inside than out. Still jet-lagged, although I slept a record 17 hours yesterday. I walked around Catania very briefly, you know, the usual, looking for fruit and water, but as it was Easter Sunday even less was open than usual. So I came back to my apartment, saw the greatest photo op of all time, which I was actually too tired to record and then went to bed at 3 pm. Usually I try to hold out until 7 or 8 but I was a mess. Even when I woke up at 8 am I was sad and felt like I still had a few hours in me. I wanted to stay in bed forever. If you had woken me up during that sleep I would have been apoplectic. I think it is less fun to sleep in if someone else is there. It's the best when no one but you knows. And your thoughts are freer. I think I was dreaming like a champ.

Anyway I hauled myself to the bus station (and have blisters on my right hand as a result) and since then everything has been swell. Well, except everything is still closed. Today's a holiday too. So I couldn't post this letter. However, during my travels this afternoon I saw exactly where I can mail it tomorrow. I think I recalled, upon getting very woozy while walking, that I had not had a decent meal since Friday night. I went into a trattoria and ordered a salad, which was not in the plan, and apparently wasn't in theirs either: they told me it was a fixed menu but made an exception. Then the sweet waiter brought me a thick slice of some sort of festive pastry. Now, as you could guess, normally I would not go in for that, but he looked so pleased to give it to me, his smile was so huge, that I couldn't bear to leave it. So there you go, you would have been proud. Also, on the plane, guess what!! On my third flight I was so out of it and hungry, that when they brought the "snack", there was a piece of smoked salmon and I ate it!! I also ate the little chocolate Easter bunny. I really amazed myself. I guess maybe I have discovered that my 3rd consecutive flight is my threshold for normal behaviour, after that all bets are off. I probably would have eaten a can of peas had it been set in front of me.

+ I should add it was excellent. Weird but ex.

Catania is a horrific place, from all I saw, and I hope never to return. Siracusa is lovely, and my landlord people are extremely nice. They picked me up, both cute as buttons, and set me up here. I can't get over how big this place is. A huge bed and even a cot. Come over! We can't watch TV but we can read in front of the blue-flamed heating unit! So let's see, are you up yet? Yes, it's 11 am your time. I am reading "Kiss and Tell" and I am teetering ~~about it~~ in my assessment of it between stickily precious and somewhat inspired. Some dude named deBotton. I am having déjà vu, did I already tell you this? Dammit.

Next is the McGuane book you gave me. I haven't seen a beach here yet. God, I hope there is one. I never used to like the beach but I converted last year. Now I only like Italian beaches. South Beach sucked. Sorry, but it did. Man I hated Miami.

[You're probably dying, at this point, for the part where I finally find a mailbox]

Mmm, nice heating unit. Sorry about my blithering penmanship. I ran this morning, it was OK, but I have scouted out where to run here. It's going to be great. The location of my apartment is perfect. In Siracusa (technically I am in Ortigia) there are Greek ruins and very old cathedrals. Today I saw a temple of Apollo. Lots of tourists here.

Human kindness holds such sway over me. Do you ever take it for granted? Particularly when you are in another country, sometimes it's like a life preserver in the shallow end, you don't see it coming, and you'll survive without it, but it's so nice to give your arms and legs a rest for a little while. Something I didn't mention in my Reggio section is a detail I love about Italian domestic architecture. Above any doorway is a window, usually 2x1 feet, and I couldn't see what the use was until I lived with Caterina (and then Raffaello). It's a way of keeping track of what people in other rooms are doing. Sound isn't always good enough, and I learned to distinguish, while in my room, whether there was someone in the kitchen, in the kitchen with the TV on, kitchen lights out but TV on, Caterina in her room with door open, Caterina in her room with door closed, bathroom etc by the various permutations of light. I learned these things despite myself. Clever Italians. Preying on human nature like that. Or catering to it, depending on your perspective. Anyway, my view right now is that there is no one in my bedroom. The window above the door is black.

O space heater of infinite warmth and good will!

Have you received my TO letter yet? I sent it on Thursday. Maybe I will sign off here, I must be boring you. Here are some addresses-you'll probably get this just as I am leaving Siracusa, so I'll leave this one off.

April 29-May 3: Me c/o
               Bed + Breakfast Lerux
               Via Callicratide 164
               Agrigento, Italy

May 3-9: Me c/o Massimo Provenza
               Via Roma 132
             Cefalu, Sicily
             90015

I am ready to send this now, sitting on the bridge between Ortigia and Siracusa proper. I took my first shower in my apartment this morning and I have to say I thought it was going rather well until I noticed something in the windows above and opposite me. They begin about 7 feet off the ground and are around 3 feet high. They are barred and triple shuttered, however they do not shut all the way. So when I happened to glance up there I saw a pair of eyes in the one slash of unimpeded glass staring back at me. Of course there are no shower curtains because this is Italy. He had climbed all the way up there! Well I gave him a dirty dirty look and he dropped away. As soon as my shower stopped all the construction work outside resumed. What's worse is I saw the guy when I left the apartment. This place is mental. I'm a perfect fit.

> Internationally yours,
> Michelle

P.S. I slept <u>16 hrs</u> last night. If I keep this up your prediction about me going comatose may come true.

Dear B,

I just checked my email and there was a quality note from you. I don't think my response was equal to it, but I tried to explain why. It was beautiful today, and I didn't do much. My mind was on overdrive last night and I must be recovering still. Wait, I think I am out of pencil lead. I have to switch.

It's much less fun in pen. I hate it. It may change the intended contents of this letter. I was visiting the duomo today and thinking how I've been a little spoiled. I would probably have to tour England's cathedrals to be impressed again. However I am looking forward to Monreale. Unfortunately stepping into Italian basilicas reminds me of previous trips. Of lighting candles for people, praying for a miracle, or just a hand on my shoulder. You should read my Rome journal, it's a little hysterical. It's a little Zelda Fitzgerald. Of course I didn't think so at the time because I had no idea who she was.

So I think I want to move to New York. If I were to ask you to help me, would you? It's very hard for me to ask this. But now is the time, I can feel it. I just wish I knew where to begin. I heard my first "basta cosi?" yesterday and it made me happy. Your note made me happy. Please write again and again. The really turned out Italian men are so stunning, and they know it. I am crazy about this book you gave me, it will be hard to put it down tonight to get to my own work. I am looking out over the water, about 1.5 hours before the sunset and everything's twinkling, especially the path of water leading right to my feet.

Yes. About moving. I've thought about school, and if I do get in, I'm not positive it's what I want. I had thought of it as a way to give myself time, as though I could bargain away 2-4 years where I would be able to concentrate more fully on writing while getting a totally unrelated degree. Is that just fooling myself? There is also the money. What I am thinking now is that if I do get in, I would defer for a year, move to NY (provided I get a job) and see how it goes, while also trying to make and save money. There is a part of me that would like the degree (do you have an MA?) and the breathing room toward maybe a PhD. Why do law professors only need a masters to teach? Neither Jen or Pat is going to teach...what was the point of their going to NYU? They needed a break. I need a break. I've been working at this job since before I graduated. I told myself I would be there a year! I have little doubt Lee will be back in NYC within the year. There are people I love very much in Toronto but it's not the kind of life I crave. Now I'm babbling. I know you don't care to hear this, sometimes I forget I'm writing a letter, it's a despicable, shameful habit.

Do you really miss me? What did I tell you in your dream? Was I nice? People here are sweet...nice nice people. I feel at home, even though there are too many tourists. That sounds ridiculous but I can't explain it. I concluded yesterday that taking a year out of my life to move here and concentrate on becoming fluent would be time very well spent. As it is I am constantly mixing French and Italian together. Disgraceful.

Pablo Neruda would vomit in his espadrilles. Fuck him though, eh?

I've been sleeping with my hair dryer. Since the propane tank ran out, it gets chilly at night. And my bed has this vague dampness about the edges. So I stick the blow dryer under the covers and crank it until I can't take it anymore. I'm not sure you would like it here. I sure like the sun, though. I'm going to find some nearby beaches and make myself as stupid as can be. Fruit-hunting has been a perplexingly fruitless ordeal. Where are they hiding it all?? Where are the peaches? Last night I had some apples that were so bad I spit one mouthful back into the paper bag. I don't get it.

B! Send grapes! Finally finally. I am here.

I think I will walk back to the apartment now. No one peeked at me showering today because I took the table cloth from the kitchen and hail Mary'ed it up over the tall tall window. It took on the first shot + now they can't see in. They tried though! When the shower started I heard them all clambering into the atrium outside my bathroom window. Sicilian bastards. How did they even know I wasn't some crazy old Mafioso who showered with a shotgun?

OK. Boys moving into turf on stealthy, black leather wings. Maybe I write more when I get home. I'll say hi to my free cake-wielding waiter for you. I know you like him because he fed me without being asked.

I guess I brought out the old Jew in him.

love,
Michelle

April 24/03

Dear B,

I write you by the shriek of my hair dryer presently blasting hot air under the covers. I was just thinking of something you said once that made me laugh, and it set off a laughing jag so prolonged that it very nearly rendered my de facto space heater obsolete. Why do I find you so funny? I don't think it would be for the reasons you may assume, i.e., "Well, because I'm one funny motherfucker!"

Last night, amid a tear of wakefulness, I was making one of a series of sleepy return trips to bed and noticed that the last sentence out of my mouth, as I was cannonballing back up and under the covers, was

"...if it's the last fucking thing I do!" Funny to catch yourself muttering like that. Today, making my way home from the Neapolis, an archeological park of Greek ruins, it occurred to me, out of where I don't know, that the first words I spoke to you were "This is not allowed!" Why am I thinking about you? You have likely forgotten me already, foul day-to-day'er! The amphitheatre in the park was stunning, but a word to the wise, don't buy a ticket to see it b/c no one checks. Save yourself 4.5€, or 12 apples, as I call them.

There is also a spectacular quarry called Dionysis' Ear, Caravaggio gave it that name after he heard about how Dionysis loved this cave because the acoustics allowed him to hear enemies from far away. Children were standing in the opening and yelling, at the prompting of their parents, and then shooting in every and any direction, screaming with actual terror when their voices came sounding back to them. I walked as deep into the huge cave as I could without getting completely spooked. It's as frightened as I have felt in a long while. Something about it was resoundingly terrible. Kind of like that inadvertent pun. I swear, I'm such a tart for the puns I can't even control them anymore.

I liked your description of the birthday card. Even better was the image of you standing in a store and laughing. You did actually laugh out loud, didn't you? You wouldn't lie to me, would you? I hope to see you laugh one day. I'm sad that I don't make you laugh more. That leaves me with nothing to do but make you cry. Despite your Paleolithic protestations to the contrary, I believe I would have a better shot at making you cry than getting a huge, satisfied laugh out of you.

Since I read your email I have been wishing I could have printed it out to read over and over. Sometimes I feel so lucky to have words from you. I'm sorry my response was so paltry but I hope my actual letters will make up for that. I don't think I will write you emails. You're hogging all my letter-writing time, you can't have emails too, Greedy Gus! Remember when you called me "greedy"? What a laugh! What a jackass you are!!

Hey, Americano, I think I wore the wrong T-shirt today, because my stock went sky-high. Somehow this T-shirt managed to give me—who you can see from photos, particularly in the blue, M. Anfinsen dress, am modestly endowed—the appearance of pin-up proportions. I had never

---

Sidebar:

One of the proudest moments of my life was when I got my friend Paul to laugh so hard, while we were jaywalking, that he doubled over, facing oncoming traffic, and I had to drag him out of the road. Lee + I had a similar moment once, but we both ended up flat out on the sidewalk. Abysmal puns were involved.

worn this shirt before, in fact removed the tag this morning before putting it on and did not check the mirror. I did not realize my mistake until I was out on the streets, and garnering much more attention than yesterday. Then I caught a glance in a car window. Ah, I see. Would you look at that.

The shower wars continue. Now when I turn the water on, the men all congregate in the atrium outside my bathroom, but instead of hollering they begin singing. When I hear a 3-part harmony there may be some kind of reward in order.

Yeah, so, the streets were lined with eyes, but it's not a contempt-filled attention, like in Reggio. Seeing a row of construction workers pleading with me, silhouetted with arms upraised on top of a building a hundred feet away until I was out of eyeshot made me laugh so hard I bumped into a parked car.

I made headway with my fruit guy. He has been very stand-offish but today asked me where I was from. I'll take what I can get from him. He's old and super cranky. Also, fruit woman (I'm still hedging my bets) let me get away with not having exact change. The world lumbers on like a zeppelin sometimes, my boy!

So where are you? I have things to tell you! Are you thinking about me? Is that what this little inkling is? People are adorable here. I don't know why I love Italians so much but they make my heart so big! Like one of those sponge tablets you drop into a glass of water, they make my heart a wreck of gigantism until it fills every corner and is good for nothing. Binged on blood. I love their faces, I love how little they are and how they think I am some huge, red-haired freak of Western engineering.

My my, B, but I don't like the way this Frank character thinks sometimes. You must not have considered my daffodilic properties when you thought of me reading this book. Numerous times I have had to throw it to the nearest flat surface (table, bed, road, bench, early Greco-Roman amphitheatre seat) and cover my furious shame with scandalized laughter. I must finish it tonight, in bed, to seal off further opportunities for public outbursts of this sort.

Tomorrow I find a patch of beach for a while and I'm going to begin Madame Bovary. I'm gonna be limb-limpeningly depressed, right? Am I right? Have you

read it? Are you my darling of ever-loving
literacy? Are you? Jesus, what's Frank
going to pull tonight? Why does he talk
about women that way? What's wrong with
this fucking guy? And Holly? Jesus. I bet
my dad's glad I haven't had an old codger
phase. Yet. Well, unless you include Kevin.
Which nobody wants to do. Because he's
tall and phoney. I could tell you things!
Why don't I ever tell people things. Do you
think it's true that you wouldn't worry
about what other people thought of you if
you knew how little they did? I sure do. I
wish I could care _more_ what people thought
of me. Might be good for the old constitu-
tion. And the bank account. Oh yeah, I
fucked up there. Somehow I failed to regis-
ter that what I am paying for a week in this
apartment is more than a month's rent at
home. Che stupido.

What are you doing? My room is damp and
the lighting is non-commital. If you were
here we would laugh. I am sorry about
wanting slices of people, I know they don't
come that way, in convenient installments
of your choosing. Nevertheless, at this
moment, were you to magically appear, we
would lie here and have eye races around
the leafy border of the ceiling fresco. And
listen to the kids packing it in, slapping the
walls and dragging their feet homeward for

the night. And we'd just be nice to each other. Because that's rare. I would trust you to be nice to me. Also rare.

And then what?

>   It's your turn, Vicar,
>   Michelle

hair falls in eye @ your request

Dear B,

Well, Madame Bovary may be even unluckier than I. She certainly is a far sight stupider. Here is my favourite passage of the day, re-written for you with every appropriate nicety of feeling:

(oh, I should say, it refers to Mme B's...misteress? It occurs to me there is no male counterpart to "mistress". Thus, I have made one up. Her misteress, who is quite the heartless a-hole.)

> (Emma) "I love you so much that
> I can't do without you—you
> know that don't you? Sometimes
> I want so much to see you that it

tears me to pieces. 'Where is he?'
I wonder. 'Maybe he's with other
women. They're smiling at him,
he's going up close to them...' Tell
me it isn't true. Tell me you don't
like any of them! Some of them
are prettier than I am, but none
of them can love you the way I do.
I'm your slave and your concu-
bine. You're my king, my idol!
You're beautiful! You're wise!
You're strong!"

He had had such things said to
him so many times that none of
them had any freshness for him.
Emma was like all his other mis-
tresses; and as the charm of nov-
elty gradually slipped from her
like a piece of her clothing, he
saw revealed in all its nakedness
the eternal monotony of passion,
which always assumes the same
forms and always speaks the
same language. He had no perception—this man of such vast
experience—of the dissimilarity of
feeling that might underlie simi-
larities of expression. Since he
had heard those same words
uttered by loose women or prostitutes, he had little belief in their

sincerity when he heard them
now: the more flowery a person's
speech, he thought, the more
suspect the feelings, or lack of
feelings, it concealed. Whereas
the truth is that fullness of soul
can sometimes overflow in utter
vapidity of language, for none of
us can ever express the exact
measure of his needs or his
thoughts or his sorrows; and
human speech is like a cracked
kettle on which we tap crude
rhythms for bears to dance to,
while we long to make music
that will melt the stars.

There you go. Ruminations on the inadequacies of language, prostitutes and bears: all your favourites!!

I don't know why I should give them to you, I don't even like you very much tonight. I believe I may begin to resent your non-presence as time goes on. So be forewarned if the letters drop off or become increasingly curt. Nothing especial to report. A very poor showing by some kid with braces on the beach. I couldn't believe it. What a mouth on this one. I spent the day lost in thought. Yes. It would be crude and, more offensively, pointless to say more than that.

I have a bad feeling I'm going to stay up too late and finish this damn book. I don't like it so much. Flaubert's a little wishy washy. I like my overheated authors ultra-overheated, like Lawrence. It's like alphabet porn. I don't think we have similar taste. Ultimately, I did not like the McGuane. In parts it was funny and some phrases were really nice, but...I don't know. Not my bag, I guess. I have nothing else to say. The bed is sticky, the cats are breaking stunning new ground with their vocal acrobatics and the vespas are vespa-ing in the distance. Plus I just sneezed. Maybe I'll add to this one. It hardly seems worth sending. Perhaps I'll like you better in the morning. Ha. Has that ever been the case?

All right. All right. Somehow I am now in a worse mood but like you better. My mood is because I am very frustrated with my jet lag, I've never had it like this. I can't sleep until 3 or 4 in the morning and I've barely been up before noon since I got here. Tuesday I have to be up by 8 and I don't know how I'm going to do it! Plus I just noticed that on the bag Erin lent me, which I take everywhere, there is not one but 2 American flags. How could I have missed that?? Great. No offense but I don't really want to walk around with American flags on my person.

There's a bit of a wind, I could do without that too! Holy crank alert, eh?

So I did stay up and read Mme Bovary to the end and it made me cry despite myself. That damned Charles, he's just like the guy in my story, poor bastard. There are parallels between Emma and the woman too. I'd like to think she's a little more sympathetic though. I've got big problems with Emma. Fucking L'heureux. Hated that guy.

The amorousness of young Italian couples always touches me. Ha ha. I find it quite "touching". There's this boardwalk, huge, with spaced out ventilation blocks and at each of the 6 of them there is always a single motorcycle and a young couple, making out like crazy. I often wonder if they don't feel like they've been put there by the ministry of tourism or at least feel terribly unoriginal, what with 5 carbon copies of themselves surrounding them. Maybe that's the appeal. Sometimes it's comforting to act out a cliché, at least when you're 17. I remember Kurt telling someone, when asked what we did the previous night, that we "made out like teenagers." It was funny because it was true. But also because I'd just turned 20 and he was only 22. Why do only teenagers get to do it? I miss those people, that group of friends I had. That was the happiest time of my life. That's the last time I remember feeling that I had a network of people around me I really liked and trusted. We had so much fun together. I loved them so much.

They were funny funny guys, and they loved me too. Did you ever have a group of friends like that? Sometimes I feel like it would hurt me to see them now. Just remind me of how different things are. And it's only going to get worse! But I'm terribly nostalgic. Been that way since I could pronounce it. Always afraid of time passing, hating change. I tell this story a lot but I remember feeling like my world was ending when my dad changed our kitchen garbage bag under the sink from a paper bag that sat on the floor of the cupboard to one of these new-fangled plastic jobs that screwed into the inside of the door. I was inconsolable, I begged him not to do it. I felt it was the end of an era. Everything was before and after for me. I was four years old.

I believe it's true that cynical people are the worst romantics and for that reason I don't believe you are a true cynic. Maybe you wouldn't argue with that. It just occurred to me that at times you come off as cynical but you are more of an optimist at heart. I am a cynic at heart and as such a hopeless, scandalous and, underneath it all, dreadfully romantic loser.

Ah, I wonder about people. I wonder about her, for one. I wonder also: Crazy Emily, Cruel to be Kind Girl and the One Who Remains Unnamed But Whom You Sometimes Think You Should Have Married, are all of these women people you were involved with? To this I imagine you saying "Whatever Bttn. Anything I have to say about this I'll say to your face." Which I take to be "fuck off" and also "we'll see if I feel like telling you when I find out how you feel in person." Which is both understandable and gay. As are most things in life, I am finding.

I take it our friend got married this weekend. Marriage. I guess that means he'll knock her up soon. I was thinking last night about that stuff. Not those two of course but babies and all that. It occurred to me, for the first time in my life I'm ashamed to say, that my dad might actually want grandchildren. I was taking the bus home after Christmas and I decided that I wouldn't rule out having a kid just so he could see it. I think it would give him some peace. Of course, it has long been my assumption that I will not marry or have kids, and I have had a good go at ensuring neither of those things will occur. But time makes liars of us all, right? I don't know. It seemed significant at the time that I was even having those thoughts. And at the last dinner my mom and bro had she made this horrible comment about my dad only having a few years left and that he should retire now and "live life". I could have killed her. Does making your family (parents) happy matter? Or is it less of an issue since they already have grandchildren? Ach. God. I can't have a kid! I _am_ a kid! But then I think, 'my mom had Chris at this age.' When I was 22 I spent most of the year marvelling over the fact that my mom got married at that age. I could barely keep my socks clean.

There's so much I don't know about those 2. Did you always know? Despite the current apartment, you know you are in it for keeps, right? I think you do.

My dad says he married my mom because he thought it would make her happy and that's all I've ever heard on the subject. And that she asked him. I have a feeling my mom's twenties may have been even worse than mine. No, that can't be. But close. Oops, here come the clouds. Hoo that's cold.

B would you believe the same kid from yesterday just sat down beside me? Come ON! I'm telling you he can't be more than 15. Braces and everything. He must have an older brother who dared him or something. This has got to be a joke. God but they start early, huh? Good thing I'm not totally undressed, like yesterday. I fucking hate when they get you like that. They sneak up on you on the beach and you suddenly feel so vulnerable because you're basically in your underpants and they're standing there dressed head to toe, as Italians always are. So you feel like "my God, I must be asking for this, I'm practically naked and he's standing there in jeans and a sweater." I don't get how Italians in this part of the world wear winter clothes in 25° weather. OK, this kid is hilarious. He's got a hearing aid and keeps blowing his nose with great honks and flourishes. I think he needs a starter course. He hasn't been prepped well.

Oh fuck off. Why doesn't he fuck off? Now he has his back up. I really resent this kind of shit. I bet he thinks "I'll sit here all fucking afternoon if I have to." And I'm thinking the exact same thing. Why should I have to move? It's a very queer feeling, however. They do make you feel like you're doing something quite inappropriate.

He just asked me for a cigarette. Go ask your mom for a fucking cigarette, pasquale! OK. Maybe I'll read now. Lee gave me a Mary McCarthy book called "The Stones of Florence", so that's next up in the queue. I'll report back with any and all brace-boy developments. Right now he seems to be starting some kind of quarry with the larger rocks on the beach. He is motioning to me, he doesn't like the fact that I am writing so much. It is depressing him. OK, he just moved a few feet closer. B. It's so boring this shit. One of the first phrases I put together in Florence four years ago was "I want to be left alone."

He just began calling me names. Weird hand signals. I told him to go away, asked him what he wanted.
Ah, thank God he just left.

Now I'm back, time to end this letter. I'm sorry I'm not a better letter-writer. I think they would really benefit from a second draft. Something tells me you would appreciate a little more craft in a letter.

Well too fucking bad.

Sometimes I write crafty letters, other times the prospect just seems tedious. Like French Manicures. A glossy approximation of what comes naturally.

Again, I have a sneaking suspicion that this is what you prefer. Well, whatever blows your man-skirt up, cowboy!

I miss you to a large and startling degree,

                         Michelle

April...uh...28

Dear B,

It seems that you have become whatever happened to my journalling tendencies, and as such I may ask you to return these to me at some point. Or at least make me some carbons.

I have just finished a tour of the catacombs of San Giovanni, they were sobering and dank. It was a good tour, not enough frescoes. Or Fresca: I'm parched! God the sun is making me her bitch today, it would have been a much better day for the beach. Part of my beak freak yesterday was also the bad weather, it drives me to distraction. No wonder I'm always such a mess at home.

Shower Wars Part the Fifth: a new low.

So there's one of those 6 inch X 6 inch windows <u>below</u> the huge, high up window that I managed to cover with a table cloth. This is one of those fun-house windows people put in basements that are like a foot thick and distort everything on the other side but still let light through. So this morning (yes, I finally managed to get up at nine), while I was drying my hair I see pubblica enemy #1 cupping his hands on the window, his eyes wide, looking right at me. Again I stop what I'm doing and stare. He leaves. I'm sure he can't see much but not positive— maybe this eye-cupping thing is the equivalent of 3-D glasses for that window. So I resume. A minute later again I see him and start to swear. He stays. I swear more. He goes. Now, I do what he does, and on my end, everything on the outside is distorted, I imagine it is for him too. So what's the deal? Again, when I leave the house I have to face this little runt and his workmen paisan. What the <u>hell</u> is that, B? Could he really be so starved for a look at a woman? Buy a magazine!

I loved your stories, crazy movie guy, bawling Adam. That one made me want to meet Adam so bad my fists balled up. Because also, what kind of a guy has three kids at 31? Some kind of guy, that's for sure. I've got to find out. Someone set that guy on "ultra breed" and then forgot where the switch was!

Did you know strawberries don't ripen? Running this morning was pure joy. I am staring at the portico of a church built in 3 C. BC.. Pretty lunette carved from stone. The ceiling caved in in 11 A.D. and was never re-built. In the distance is this huge, cone-shaped structure that houses a statue of the Madonna that was said to cry real tears. You can see this thing from anywhere in the city. I am glad I started here, it's a lovely place. Oh my God, the girls on the playground swings beside me can't be more than 11 or 12 and are smoking. One of them has a voice like the girl from the Exorcist in mid-projectile puke. At first I heard someone chanting obscenities and assumed it was a crazy old lady but looked over and saw this girl with thick glasses and a tight pink shirt swooping away on the swing set.

I have hope of letters arriving for you this week, then I will feel more comfortable dropping off the radar as I know there will be a fairly steady flow.

Listening to our guide, who gave the tour in Italian and then in English, I grew forlorn. I want to speak Italian! I could listen to him forever. Then hearing his voice in English, it was grievously inferior. I tried hard to follow the Italian version, and did OK. Is being fluent in another language a goal or even a distant desire of yours? Maybe I shouldn't have dropped out of the school last year. Nah. I did the right thing.

Did you like my aphorism in the last letter about time making liars of us all? What does time make of the people who are already liars? Here's what time makes of you: "oh he's a good egg. A 3-minuter."

Uh oh, mewling child alert. "La la! La la!" Tell that cursing brute in tight jeans to shut up, there's a child riding some sort of mallard over here! Let her ride the mallard unmaligned! God, what is that crazy girl saying? Uh oh, crazy girl just approached mother and babe but her cell phone rang just in time. Maybe it was you calling to tell her to put a sock in it.

Thank you for being such a prince last night. I mean it, you're the only one that I know will come through like a champ.

There's a store right behind me with a huge

sign that says "Orange Family Store". Should I go in there and demand repatriation or at least some informal adoption procedures? I'd settle for mascot and fruit priveli~~d~~ges. I can <u>NEVER</u> spell that word properly.

About the catchphrase of the trip, so far I think there are 3 front-runners. "Dové vai?" (Where are you going) "Dové loggia?" (Where do you live/where is your home/where are you staying) and one I seem to be getting a great deal but don't understand why: "Aspetta!" (wait!) Everyone's telling me to wait, though in my opinion other directives would be more appropriate. Yesterday, beach boy said it over and over, everything was "aspetta"—to cross the street, to look at something, to make a decision. He asked me if I played sports, which I thought was sort of charming and awkward. Then he took my hand and put it on his stomach, which I could feel through his shirt was sectioned up like a pan of sweet rolls. No Molson Muscle there, boy. But who puts a girl's hand on their stomach to show off? Italian boys. He's in the military, a peacekeeper in Bosnia.

Here comes Celia on a 2-wheeler with training wheels. There is nothing bloody cuter than an Italian little girl quibbling with her father about strategies for leaving the playground. What a little coquette.

The Stones of Florence is good, but isn't there something acrid about Mary McCarthy to you? She seems like she'd be a horrible person.

Why do you say AG is a bad person? That's disappointing. I loved his book and from it surmised that he would be decent company and maybe even a decent man. Tell me why he's not, as a fellow Canadian I demand to know why you slandered him. What did he read? Nobody ever asks me to read things. That's because I live in stupid Toronto.

It's hard to be good. Hey, where did I hear that before. I think I wrote something...I forget. Anyway, here's two lines I saw on another page in here:

> My love was an afterthought,
> the knotted heart of laughter's lot.
> Your love was a harbinger,
> a rabbit on an open plain.

Oh God, here comes old Celia, still pouting and twisting her poor dad. Would you like a daughter?

Italians aren't fat. Honest. Remember when

that poor waiter fed me cookies and sweet wine? It had the strangest taste. It slipped by you but then ducked its head back around the corner with a melting smile.

Italian pigeons <u>are</u> fat! I think it's a point of pride for the people.

OK. Basta. I will start the walk home now. I need to buy a bra on the way. I feel that if this is my journal-by-proxy you're going to have to put up with stuff like that. Because my journals are exactly that banal. Ha.

Oh my God. More kids, these two a bro and older sis. She led him into the field below the lunette and initiated a kind of jumpy, jiggle-kneed pas de deux. Like, "Look! Something pretty! We must bounce together in tribute!"

That stuff kills me.

> Killed by killing cuteness,
> Michelle

This single 'Ha.' thing I got from you. I don't like it but now I can't stop.

Also, can I steal the thing you said about big waves across small spaces for my story?

April 29

Dear B,

You can never underestimate the effect of voices. The power they have to soothe or grate is absolute. The women on the second leg of my bus trip to Agrigento were an 11 on the Star Frit Solutions power-grater scale. Here is something I wrote to Lee with regard to the boys I was stuck beside on the plane, and it goes triple for the chatterboxes of Catania: I have run the gauntlet of hall of shame seatmates—fat lumber-sawers, sweaty pervs, suspected terrorists, colicky babies, puking old ladies, my <u>mother</u>—but never has my burden caused me to look upon the possibility of hari kiri via butter knife more fondly than that I was laden with last week.

Not only were there 4 of these people, but the ringleader, the one with the voice that could shred paper, stood up, turned around (she was in front of me, the rest dotted in various seats on a par with me and behind) and began basically shouting in my face, so she could be heard by all. The shouting continued for 3 hours, broken only when one of them took a cell phone call (and they all took several) and then the shouting was limited to the callee, the rest respectfully ceasing to talk so that one of their own could hear herself think, but moreso, I suspect, so that they could better glean the caller's identity, if not the contents of the conversation. Do you notice my handwriting getting more erratic the more I talk about this? Holy cannoli!

But at last I am in Agrigento. It seems lovely so far, but the bus ride here really took it out of me. I've got a bitchin' headache and I'm hungry. I am waiting for my apartment guy to return + take my money so I can turn in for the night. He has a speech impediment, a grave kind of stammer that only kicks in at certain moments. I'm trying to hash it out. He also drove me away from the address I thought I was staying at. I didn't ask. Now I'm somewhere else. He wanted to go for gelato but I said just

→ Do you know I didn't even get his name?

water please. Then he left and I couldn't get my door open so I had to call him and ask him to come back. It made me feel pretty dumb. Did you find your wallet? Did my letters find you?

This place is spectacular, the streets are teeming with interesting-looking people. God, when Italians dress up it's something. Really fucking sharp. I really missed you on the stuffy stuffy bus. I could have used a laugh. I was trying to be very still and use as little oxygen as possible. It was a double decker! I think that was a first for me. Makes you kind of woozy taking those Sicilian wows in the road. Tonight I start "Earthly Powers", have you read it? How's work? Busy? Boring? Are you scrabble cheating on me?

Tomorrow I go to the Valle du Tempii. They say that these are the most spectacular Greek ruins outside of the Parthenon. And I've never been to Greece so they'll be the best I've seen, that's for sure.

I'm thinking of extending my trip. I'd like to spend time in Rome. It would be my third year in a row in Rome, I seem to really love it. Even more than Florence.

My dad has informed me that in June he is

going to Eastern Europe. Another <u>tour</u>.
Barf. I guess we have officially entered the
touring years. Do your parents tour? Do
you parlez-vous? That last was a question
posed to me at the wedding last year by a
Harvard medical student that really made
me laugh. Americans are funny.
You're funny.

There certainly are—woops, here's my guy,
hang on. Uh oh, there are more people
here. A man and a woman. They are staying down the hall.

April 30

Dear B again. It is the next day now, everything went wacky there for a while. I am in
a place called San Leone and waiting for
the bus home on a little patio with bright
blue plastic seats. There is a beautiful
beach here and I put off the temple until
tomorrow. After much taking of buses and
inquiring of old people I found the beach.
One old lady became very proprietary about
my success in this matter and gave me
directions over and over on the bus. I ended
up going a full route of Bus #1 due to the
ill-informed directions of my host. But so
did the old senora! Then, as I got off at the
Valley of the Temples, as she advised, nay,

incanted, ~~and~~ she continued on. As I was waiting for bus No 2, I saw her, half an hour later, passing by on yet another go around, on the same bus. She was nothing compared to the old guy who sat beside me. Adorable. I could have crushed him like a cracker. When he got off he gave me the old elbow and a short "ciao!" as if we'd been friends since Dieppe and would meet again like this in the afternoon. The bus debacle I didn't mind because it was a lovely ride into the Agrigento lowlands, and I got a preview of the temples, plus I love observing Italian bus culture, i.e. old ladies who ride them to be social and the lovely, convivial chatter that gilds them. For Italians I think silence is death. The old ones are the only strain you see without cell phones. I can't imagine what the rest of them did before their invention.

Funny thing about my host, whose name I still have not registered...when I told him I was only staying for 4 nights, not 5, he was upset and said that Saturday was his birthday party and he had planned on me being there—as if I had received the invite in the mail weeks ago. I just met him! Also, he seems to want to hang out, I feel this may be a problem. I am not looking forward to going home and half-expecting him to barge in the apartment at any moment, as he did twice this morning, asking after my plans. However, here is the funny thing: I guess while showing my roommates around—while I was in my room—he peeked in the bag I had set on the fridge and saw it contained the strawberries I bought in Siracusa. This morning, during visit #2, I was in the shower. I was very annoyed because I didn't much care to be seen post-shower by him, as there wasn't much of a towel to get me from the bathroom to my room. I thought 'Oh Christ, is he going to stay here until I'm done?' Anyway he yelled good-bye to me as I was washing my face. So I get into my room and see he has left 2 containers of strawberries on my desk with a note. Very sweet, no? I continue getting ready, dress, pull stuff together and go to the kitchen to get the diet coke I bought yesterday from the fridge to take with me. I open the fridge and see that he has covered the entire top shelf with containers of strawberries.

I laughed my bloody head off. What a kookoo! It occurred to me yesterday that I could have been close to my premonition of an Agrigento death occurring. I thought for a moment, ~~that~~ while in his car, with this strange guy, that I could be on my way to butchery. But I did not remember that Agrigento was the scene of the death I described to you. So far, still alive. I am very out of touch with the news, what the hell's happening?

And where's the goddamn bus? It was supposed to be here 15 minutes ago.

I was very content last night to sleep, after reading the first 50 pages of Earthly Powers. Its brilliance is making me a little heartsick. That's the way I'd like to write. His instincts are impeccable, his syntax whippet lean and well-proportioned. It's driving me a little crazy how good he is. It is a total joy to read. I have 500 huge, tinily-printed pages to go and already I am dreading the end. Is Burgess still alive? I've got to start reading all of his books right now!

What are you reading, pop tart? You are at work right now, 11:45 am.

Such a lovely beach. When I closed my eyes the waves coming in felt like they were going to overtake me every time. Some weird acoustics thing I attribute to the breakers on either side of me.

Some freaky palm trees. Looks like a normal palm tree swallowed an armadillo and is having trouble digesting it. OK. This is getting retarded. I can't write, rapid devolution. I'll try reading now until the dastardly bus comes. Too, if you don't stand out on the street and wave the bastards down they will not stop for you. You gotta earn a ride on the big orange crawler. God, is this enough of a letter to send? Are you sick of these yet?

      Are you?
           Michelle

PS.
Oh my God! At the second I finished the right leg (my right) who drives up on motorcycle but apartment guy. I am 10 miles from home! How does this happen?? He is inside now getting ice cream. Come over!!

15 minutes later: woops, I think we just had our 1st fight.

May 1

Dear N'dugu,

I wish I could send you a picture with this letter of the spot where it was begun. I am at the foot of a huge Greek temple, sitting on a rock atop a cliff that overhangs a stretch of farmland before giving way to the sea. And I am wondering why I just scaled a mother of a hill in order to reach the "valley" of the temples. Also, I keep getting vertigo because there is nothing standing between me and oblivion should the 4 year old tyrant belligerizing behind me get it into his head to give me a swift kick. My God. It's the most ridiculously breathtaking sight. You never have to wonder why the Greeks chose the sites they did to colonize. This one seems kind of far from the sea.

But then again those catacombs I was in the other day were originally Greek aquaducts. So who am I to quibble with the greatest civilization in human history? It's photo op central, I am regularly enlisted to take snaps of sweaty couples and flushed families so please excuse the inevitable breaks in my train wreck of thought.

My host is making me move to a new location tonight and I am not happy about it. What's his damage anyway? Last we left off he was miffed because I flatly refused a ride back into town on his bike and also nixed plans for the evening. He thinks I am a crazy loner. He catches on fast. You know that Dandy Warhols song?

"I could own her, that crazy loner,
If I found my way to Minnesoter"

You said that you sent me a letter, I wonder to where. To Cefalù? Will Massimo hand it to me when I roll into town? That will be very surreal and quite possibly the best thing ever.

I am still marvelling over 'Earthly Powers', I kind of wish we were both reading it so we could mind meld or at least talk about certain passages. A funny thing is happening, all of the books I have been reading so far

are beginning to talk to one another.
Recurrences, picking up dropped threads.
It's amazing. Oh God! Spider in my skirt!
Oh God! Ancient white spider in my skirt!

Oh shit. That was one of those times when
trying to get it off you only makes it worse
and in fact moves the spider from the outside of your skirt to the inside. I think
wrestling myself over this cliff to rid myself
of the intrepid octoped would have been
worth it. Didn't come to that. Let's have
more of that Dandy Warhols song to get
back on track:

> In a slumber, I'm sawin' lumber
> I saw my baby dance a latin number
> With her shirt off, man her skin's soft...

There, that's better.

So yeah, massive synchronicity in my read-
ings. I'm diggin' it. Next up is the Elkin,
we'll see if it continues.

Oh B, maybe we should always live in far
apart countries so we can write letters. I
anticipate yours rather desperately. I wonder what it will be like. I had my first
dream about Lee ever two nights ago. I
think he will be relieved to hear that. He's a
good boy. I wish he weren't so unhappy

there — there is a goofy ice cream truck waaaay down in the valley, looks like a pink potato bug trundling along, but it is playing this dopey dance music at such a crank that I can hear it from here.

Hm. A flock of birds just shot-putted out from some hidden den. Flung out like confetti. Or a shot put. Or confetti. Who can decide, really.

Ambulances haunt this place, I've heard 2 sirens already. It is an artery buster's paradise, what with all the oldies and parasols and taxing foothills. Come when you're young! Why do so many old people wait to travel? When I imagine them seeing things I am seeing and have seen at the end of their lives I get very upset. It shouldn't be an afterthought. Not that I'm so well-travelled, seeing as I keep coming back here. But if I could, I would. I guess they would offer the same argument but I don't buy it. If I can manage a big trip a year so can they. You mentioned, in that big email I didn't much grasp, about JA and the questions his writing (or perhaps more correctly subject matter and approach) raised for you. You said that there are certain things a writer should take for granted in his or her reader, and that is that everyone has felt powerful, or felt embarrassed, or come, or travelled. I didn't say it at the time but I disagree with this both on its merits, as you would say, and in its theoretical application to a more elegant school of writing. I don't think you can or should take those things for granted. Oh Fuck! Spider alert! I don't think those little bastards like it when I try to get all substantive. MotherFUCKER I hate spiders.

As a reader, the most compelling experiences I have had have been excellent portraits of things I haven't experienced, or things I have thought of experiencing but never have, or, or. What oft was thought but ne'er so well expressed, yes, but also what oft was envisioned, if not necessarily experienced. Why are teenagers the largest market for music, film, etc.? Because they're curious. I guess I would quibble more with your exemplars, touchstones of universal human experience. I remember as a little kid putting it to my parents what they thought was something, the one thing every human being on earth has found pleasure in. I can hardly believe my precocity now, but I wanted to connect everyone, or at least one experience that I could know was universal the next time I had it. They went back and forth for a while, quibbling, like me, over details and standards and possibilities. A few candidates were tabled, but I rejected generalities like "food", I wanted specifics. Of course it came down to the bathroom, but even there my dad found a [SPIDER!!] loophole. I don't think they withheld talk of sex out of delicacy. Of course children don't generally have sex, and I think at least half of all grown women have never come. Ultimately there was nothing. And that stuck with me for a long time, obviously, while they both agreed there had to be something, neither of them could give it up.

I don't know where I'm going with this anymore, that damn spider has me all preoccupied. How about an Earthly Powers quote of the day to cleanse the palate?

(Man ripping into his gay lover, an author)

> "Oh, listen to the transmuter of experience into deathless words. Read that somewhere, they didn't mean you, dear. Miss Mouse, writing about what he won't do, living by poxy, proxy that is."

Here is another, this is the old author @ 81:

> "There were cases showing off jade, ivory, glass, metal "bibelots" or objêts d'art". How the French terms, admit-

ting their triviality, somehow cleansed them of it. The tangible fruits of success. The real fight, the struggle with form and expression, unwon.

Oh my God — the "real" fight? I was thinking like an author, not like a human, though senile, being. As though conquering language mattered. As if, at the end of it all, there were anything more important than clichés. Faithful. You have failed to be faithful. You have lapsed, or fallen, into infidelity. I believe that a man should be faithful to his beliefs."

Dear B, there is a stripe of my neck that seems to have less sensation than the rest, can you do something about that? It's like I'm touching it through Saran Wrap™. The tops of my wrists and hands are burnt and it's all your fault. Too much writing to you in the sun. I am now on the far side of the valley. It really is a pretty gruelling round of ruin-gawking. My conclusion: I'm not a big fan of ruins. In Florence and Rome I couldn't get enough of the cathedrals, in fact after a few days I knew I had to pace myself—only 1-2 churches/day—lest I fall into a rapture and check myself

into the nearest nunnery. I guess when
you're raised with it it's always in you,
ready to pounce. Do you feel that way?
What's your relationship with your religion?

At the temple of Zeus there was a clutch of
Italian kids who hopped the fence and were
freely traipsing the temple, despite, well,
the fence, but also the hundreds of people
docilely taking photos and pointing from
the <u>outside</u> of the fence. When a French
tour guide finally ordered them out they
relented but then mocked him openly all
the way down the hill. "how <u>dare</u> he tell us
to remove our feet and motorcycle helmets
from the ancient temple?" Fucking
Franchese. I think I should buy a new
watch. This girl on the bus had one I
admired very much. It had a thick black
band and a big square face. Looked like an
old man's watch. My watch is retarded, as
you know, and was some sort of booby
prize my mom got for making excessive
purchases at a Paris boutique.

Yuck flies everywhere here.

A dumb thing happened a few minutes ago.
Ask me about it. Ask about the boys and
the camera. It happened in Rome once too,
now that I think about it. But those boys
were German and actually boys.

All right, another thrilling installment
burns itself into flaky ashes.

Again, I look forward to the next place.
Agrigento has been just fine. No doubt I'll
write you again tomorrow, I've acquired
quite as taste for it. Again, I wish they were
better letters. I can never get how I feel here
down on paper properly. And those who
can't, dither. Dither and thither, I take my
leave for now.

Why are all the stores closed today? It's
Thursday! There's no rhyme or reason to it,
that's my objection. I get upset when I can't
count on certain standbys. Oh, also, about
turning down that motorcycle ride. Is it
considered unadventurous if you really
don't feel like doing it? Sometimes I lie
awake parcelling out my adventurousness
or lack thereof. Should I have done it anyway on the off chance that something
adventurous would happen, and damn the
consequences of giving a faulty impression
in the process? Can you choose your
adventures or does that make them com-
promised? I think I only take chances when
there is a good chance of reward. I may
have it all wrong. I curse my nature sometimes, and yet am not altogether miserable.
Always wishing for the other, wondering

what I'm missing. You should come to Italy.
You could say you're being 'adventurous'
and isn't that what she loves about you?

>   Cheekily,
>   Michelle

May 2/03

Dear B,

For both getting on a plane that is not bound for Italy and leaving New York, where letters for you are, by contrast, faithfully bound, today, you get

        NIENTE

               Michelle

May 3/03

Dear B,

Well, so, my embargo lasted a whole 24 hours. Are you sick of this paper yet? Sorry it's not something a little more aesthetically appropriate, you know, stark yellow or with little Murano decals.

I am on a train to Palermo. Trrrain. Love the train. What was I thinking on the bus? The train is where I belong. I suppose you will be on the autotrain soon. I had a most unpleasant dream about you last night, must have been going along with my general mood B-wise yesterday. We had quite a row last night before I slept! Which was unlike most nights, where I whisper things to the wall until I pass out.

+ you can open windows!

I didn't see Ruggero (finally!) before I left, in fact the last I saw of him was our fight in San Leone. That's not quite true, about half an hour later, I was on the bus at a stop sign and I noticed someone pull up beside my window. I looked down and it was him, smiling up at me rather devilishly. Then he zoomed off and the bus ate his dust. How did he do that? He's like magic.

So Palermo. My dad gave me a good pop culture reference but spoiled Godfather III entirely for me by telling me that at the end, the part where the entire family is mowed down was shot on the steps of the Palermo opera house. Weird that they went all the way to Palermo to shoot a NY scene.

Some old guy above my apartment pukes out the window like clockwork every night. It's really awful.

I saw something sweet on the beach yesterday, there was a family, 4 kids, mom + dad, parents looked late 30's/early 40's. 3 girls, one boy who was clearly going to be gay. Anyway, the mom was on her stomach, tersely working through the pages of a magazine, I couldn't see the husband as he was lying on his back beside her and her body was blocking him, ~~but~~ all I saw was his left hand, which he was grazing around the small of his wife's back, up the slope of her rear. He was sort of lazily circling his fingertips, you could see so much affection in the gesture. The wife paid absolutely no mind and I was wishing I could see the husband to see if his eyes were closed and he was on autopilot or if he was looking at her, diligently vying for her attention. He never let up, 5 minutes, 10 minutes, I was hypnotized by it and finally had to force myself to look away. It really got me. 4 kids and still it was obvious he was crazy about her.

I saw the same old lady who helped me the other day on the bus. Of course she was taking the #7 again. Same 4 black bobby pins in her white yellow hair.

I was wondering, if I ever get to meet your friend B----, the filmmaker, do you think it would be OK if I...well, last night I was going through a list of alternate names, Buck, Bob, Bubba, Brandon...and then I blurted out "Bingo" and there commenced a laughing fit of old Jew proportions. Please can I call him Bingo? I will ask him, of course, but do you think he'll mind? There's just no way I can call him by his name. It goes without saying that as far as our purposes go he is Bingo.

Agrigento: not as charming as Siracusa, my fruit guy was swell. I made the mistake of going to another guy for peaches and he totally fucking swindled me. I don't know why I let it happen. They were bad too.

Pretty countryside. Chatter-free train car. I'm in heaven. This morning I ran early, it's Saturday, and I expected fewer people around, but at 8:30 am there were kids everywhere, getting the jump on hangin out and making out. I am again surprised at the young young kids smoking. I feel like telling them "Look, you guys have got it all over the rest of the world's tweens without the cigarettes!" I don't know how they do it but the kids here are so damn cool. They don't seem to have a gawky stage and if they do nobody told them.

> About cool kids: to me there is nothing cooler than seeing a group of greased up, jean-jacketed, motorcycle straddling teenage boys greeting each other with double-cheek kisses. That kills me.

Funny that you wrote me about JA when 3 letters ago I was on about him again. That has happened several times. You may not notice it because of the time delay but it has.

What are you doing, B? Where are you now? Why don't I have nice handwriting that would make you like me more? Who lives in that tiny stone shack on the side of that huge, green, and otherwise barren hill?

—TUNNEL!—

. . .

Whew. Those always give me pause. You too, eh? Although I am still enjoying Earthly Powers I'm

—T!—

oh, little one

not sure if any book could live up to its first 50 pages, much less a 600 page one. I want to do a steam roller all the way down one of these velvet dunce cappy hills. They look like they've got

—Oh!—

tremendous give. Do you have tremendous give?

I'm like the radio, I cut out during tunnels.

Alora, I return to you some time later, on another train, this one for Cefalù. There are two rowdy boys in my car. I wish I could understand them. Waiting in the Palermo station I saw the two most beautiful boys, they greeted each other with the two kisses I mentioned earlier and I had to stifle a swoon. I love train stations too. I maintain that the Florence train station is one of the most rewarding people-watching hubs in the world. What are these dudes <u>talking</u> about? Last time I picked up my email there were some very nice notes from strangers about Basta Cosi, that made me feel good. I'm still waiting for my small press guy to give me some hard information. He insists that he's very interested in me but is in the midst of some crisis or another. I trust no one, as you know.

I haven't had a chance to read your Sly Stone excerpt yet, corrupted or no...but it said "a fiction" does this mean you are not writing a biography? The only thing I can compare it to in approach (and please forgive me) is "Blonde", that Joyce Carol Oates thing—is it like that? Also, you didn't tell me you had a book already finished. Jesus Christ.

How does the paperback grow? Are you using your month extension well? I just called my man in Cefalù...he sounds nice, and in case there was any confusion, he told me as much. He said, in response to my arrival time of 15:45, "OK, I'll meet you

at the train station, I'm the nice guy." As if this should be sufficient delineation in a crush of train station men.
So I guess I'll look for the nice guy.
Oh, here we go. Il treno partenza.

I just paid 2€ for a pop in the station. Scandalous.
Every time I put my foot up a condottore comes by. It's like they have radar!

Oh B, wouldn't it be fun to hang out. Now is another one of those moments when I think it would be perfect if you were here. Something about being trapped in motion brings it on, I guess.

A girl has been thrown into the shriekish mix behind me and the boys are reaching riotous excitement levels. I can hardly blame them, can I. My ear drums, however...

Wincing, but tolerantly,
Michelle

P.S. I am not "all hot" for feedback on my letters. I'll take it, but I don't remember a word of them, and suspect them all of crushing dullness.

May 4/03

Dear B,

A sandy one for you. There may be blotches←suntan lotion, please, I request forgiveness in advance. Massimo's directive to look for the "nice guy" couldn't have been more apt, as he would be the cardboard cutout of same. He rolled up to me on his bike and flagged down a cab to take me to the apartment. As he was loading my suitcase into the trunk he said "So this is the famous Michelle Orange." I think I went green for half a second, thinking maybe apartment renters all over Italy have some kind of underground network or that maybe he is a google savant of your calibre...then I realized he's just the kind of young gun sales guy who says stuff like that. All the young groovy Italians seem to be taking a piece of the Italian real estate pie. Anyway, the apartment is bloody awesome. I had to take pictures of it it's so cool. If you came you could even have your own room.

I unpacked a bit and then walked down the huge hill my apartment is perched on to look at the city. Oh, did I mention there is a swimming pool I can use? So I love it here, it reminds me of Tropea. It's pretty tourist trappy but I can live with that. The duomo has a gorgeous, scary mosaic of "Jesus Pantocrator". Isn't it funny that two people from different countries can meet in a third one simply by saying "Meet me on the steps of the duomo at 1 pm." That's what Dimme and I will do on Tuesday.

Just now my cheap bikini top broke. The clasp. So good-bye red white and blue. Any requests for the new one?

There is an English couple in the apartment below mine right out of a Mike Leigh movie. They have a little baby. Oh shit that reminds me, I had the baby dream again last night. This time my baby started talking to me. Giving me advice. Some of it not half bad.

Heated volleyball match taking place here. Of course they can't help themselves in the tendency to let it devolve into a soccer game every few minutes before checking their natures and valiantly resuming the attempt to be Californian.

Who wants to be Californian anyway? I see someone who really needs to get out of the sun.

Let us return, however, to the issue of the bikini. I am particularly sad because, despite being cheaply made, and busting at the slightest sign of impatience with its convoluted clasp, it was the very cute and equally rare combination of string top and—if you are familiar with the term—"boy cut" bottom. Hard to find. I'm in the duomo piazza again, listening to French tour guides...again.

I love listening to native Italians lead French tours, and somewhat inexplicably pride myself on being able to pick out an Italian accent in French. Yesterday I horned in on a French explanation of the Norman mosaic. Gee this is a big tourist town, eh? But that's OK, sometimes tourists are comforting to me.

Last night I met a girl from Taiwan, also

staying in my apartment complex. It was
the most English I've spoken in two weeks.
It was like a damn broke or something.
Man I just got shafted on this pop I'm
drinking. Hate the shaft. I'll show these
dirty tourist-trappers! I see a man with
James Dean's hairline. Bit of the profile too.
Wowza.

Why are there no black tourists?

Anyway, Taiwan girl, who speaks English
very well, was super cool. We talked for a
while. She is also here for a month, and
knows Massimo because he used to work at
her firm in Taiwan! Guess he gets around,
huh? I...ew. Oh man. There is a rooster
close to my apartment, or a farm I suppose
I should say. I awoke to clear, prolonged
rooster crows at the crack of dawn. Or half-
awoke. I must have attributed it to the baby
dream because it wasn't until I heard spo-
radic rooster action while getting ready that
I recalled the earlier ones. I thought
"Goddammit, I <u>was</u> woken up by a rooster!"
Why do clichés always surprise us when
they surface?

Have you ever been woken by a rooster? I
can't believe I can now say I have. I also
killed one of the most mutative insects I
have ever seen last night. The first, while

abominable, I at least recognized, but the second was like something out of "Scanners".

Today passes under the shadow of my conviction that I am getting fat. It may be the heat, making everything stick to me, making _me_ stick to me, but it seems there is just far too much of me. Elch.

So, B. How are ya? What's new? I have been very negligent in further work on writing. It will pick up, though. I don't push it. I really should push it. That reminds me, thank you for responding to my rather plaintive plea for transplantation help. As to what kind of work I'm looking for, I'd say writing work, but not advertising. Editing I would take. Perhaps journalism although not TV news and I don't have a degree. My prof. experience is in kids TV, and new media, it's true, but I got a pretty broad base, in terms of production, directing and writing...editing etc. And I'm not into kids stuff at the moment. I need a change. Magazine work might be good experience. I'd write for TV...mainly writing is the thing. Like Johnny, of course, I harbour dreams of landing the great TV job writing jokes. But the main thing is writing, and at least a modicum of creativity involved. I have a bad feeling it may be pie in the sky for a

Toronto girl to think this way, but I would be pretty averse to taking a grunt work job. I'm too old for that, and probably too proud. Why can't I just win the lottery and set up shop somewhere, grow snow peas and write?

Anyway. That's what I have to say about that right now. Lovely boy looking at me. Think he's gay. That's what my dad would say. Did you know that my dad is secretly homophobic? Even though or perhaps because his two best friends and one close colleague turned out, late in life, to be gay? Sometimes he says things that really irritate and shock me. And it's not getting any better with age I'll tell you whut.

Oh my God, the cutest little boy just approached me. He stood at my table, looking down, holding a flower, until I looked up at him. Then he raised his eyes and had this splitting grin on his face. I smiled back and he waved the flower, we both started laughing and he turned, elated, and ran like the wind back to his table.

What a face on that kid. What a little doll.

Erin is wondering what our apartment situation will be and I have no idea what to tell her. Op, aggrieved-looking British family incoming. No one can look peevish like a pale little British lad. Perpetual confusion mingled with horror on their faces. They look so vulnerable. Man, I saw this couple with their little baby, freshly stood upon his legs, walking down a side-street. The streets here are a nightmare of lumpy rocks, about lemon-sized and very irregular. Anyway, they were letting this tiny baby try walking down the street, and every time the thing would take a terrible fall they'd go "Op!" and put him on his feet. It was terrible. I was having a hard time keeping my ballast...right as I passed he took another slappy dive to the stones. Poor little baby. Stupid parents. I hated them. Take that fucking kid away from them!

So are you on a train, bus, plane or car right now? What are you reading? "Earthly Powers" has hit a bit of a lull. I guess it was inevitable. Getting very dogmatic. Super political. Not as funny. Not as acerbic. Still good though.

Sundays. So lazy here. There is a vast boardwalk and a very, very cheesy beach. Crowded as hell today. I don't think I will find a fruit market open. Why didn't I remember to buy more yesterday? There was a passage in EP last night that was almost word-for-word what my dad said to me in part of our radio interview. It was about memory and the mind's perversity. Let me try to find it. It reminded me of the lamentably bad "Tic Tac Toe,' that Dino B-side of yore. OK:

"I remember the American neighbor of this film rather well, at least the songs in it. 'Breakdown' for example:

> Write a little note
> On your toes
> Don't forget to dot the i
> Look at what you wrote
> Goodness knows
> It's easy as pie
> Let's do the Breakaway
> Get hot and shake away...

And so on. What is the human memory playing at, that it can hold such inanities and forget great lines by Goethe?"

Funny, huh? Simpering English boy now chastising his mother: "It's...not...YOURS!!"

Oh, my Italian boy just went over to their table to get in on the action, or smooth things over. He beamed a smile all around and placated them temporarily. Then his mom came and dragged him back into neutral territory. Now the 2 boys are playing a game I can only describe as "boo!" It transcends all language barriers.

My. Heart. Is. Going. To. Burst. This is too sweet even for me. They jump up and down together and go "boo! boo! boo! boo!" and then collapse into each other's arms. Italian boy just threw an ear-hitting (self-inflicted) twist into it. This confused the already confused and pained English boy and he promptly face-planted, calling an end to the festivities with tears and blurry pointing here and there.

I'm telling you, when that kid smiles, his face blooms, it must take up half his face. Funny how some smiles are so enchanting. Do you think the aesthetic perfection of children is the meant to inspire love in their fathers? ~~It's been~~ A mother's love seems to be taken as a given. "Taken as a given"? It must be time for my meds. It's so cool seeing these two kids try to communicate. Maybe they are cute so that if their parents die or abandon them other adults will be helpless to do other than take them in and love them.

← but men are more visually co-erced

I go now. Maybe more later. The Chermans are closink in on me...Achtung! Achtung! It's the rearguard coming back!

OK. Next day. Hey, guess what my mom's response to NYU giving me the velvet shaft was? "Whatever will be will be." She's full of those, I should really start writing them down.

Last night I told myself stories, one was about a man named Boo and the other, a David-inspired one, was about a boy who dreamed of hot dogs, but was indignant that in his dreams the hot dogs were always naked when everyone knows he likes his with ketchup and mustard etc. He didn't understand it, and sets out to convert his dream hot dogs to the more appetizing kind. I am in an old man hot zone, and one just asked me if I was writing him a love note. "Scrivereme passione?" Funny old men. One is practically in my lap right this second. We're quite a pair.

I'm going to send this now. I've got to go buy a new bathing suit.

>			Clock striking noon,
>				Michelle

May 6/03

Dear B,

We'll call this one the "waiting for Dimme" letter. He seemed incapable of narrowing his time down any further than "between 13h and 16h". That's not so good eh? I don't have anything too interesting to report, other than the fact that I think I broke the washing machine last night. It was a curiously trendy-looking apparatus. Cute, small, a mini-version of those vintage coke bottle windows cyclopsing out. But completely inscrutable in function. When I finally got it working I left, returning half an hour later to find it still churning away in these strange, petulant little bursts. I reset it on rinse to get it overwith and went back inside. 2 hours later I go down to retrieve the stuff and it seems finished but I can't get the damn door open. I tried twice and on the third go the handle came off in my hand. I don't know what it is with me and Italian handles, its like I've got brute strength or something. Anyway, now my laundry is trapped inside. And I'm afraid. I don't want to be a bad guest! I could hardly sleep I was so anxious about it. I just called Massimo and he hurriedly explained the labrynthine sequence of events that will open the door, not fully grasping that I was telling him I had broken it. I wonder if they will make me pay, that would be disastrous! Why didn't he tell me that you had to turn the machine off, unplug it, do the hokey pokey and then wait for 60 seconds before the door would deign to open? I hate being in trouble. What a cheap piece of shit. Looks great though. Much like my bikini.

I am also slightly annoyed at the discovery, upon checking my email for Dimme's erstwhile ETA, that you have not written me anything since Thursday. It's Tuesday! I know you went to Godforsaken Florid-a but still. This is more than I can bear. Plus a bird just shit on me. Honest to God. Now I <u>know</u> you don't miss me and if I could stop writing these motherfucking letters I would. Since I didn't realize I would be waiting up to 3 hours I didn't bring a book. Curses. I think I am actually falling into a bad mood! No, that can't be. What do I care if you don't write me? Don't miss me?

This morning I finally finished Earthly Powers. All in all I'd say it's magnificent. Though flawed, they are at least interesting flaws. So I am all ready to start the Elkin, which I should be doing right now. Which novella is your favourite? The bear one?

Oh who cares, you suck. Everything better be OK. I'll feel like an even bigger buttmunch if some sort of problem impeded you. How many more appendixes are there to rupture in your immediate orbit? That stuff never happens to me. I'm always the one inflicting rupture. Usually to handles of various permutations.

My mom flew to London yesterday. She will visit her cousin the lute player and also buddy of the oh-so-erudite John Lahr. I hope to meet that guy someday. One part of Earthly Powers that was great was his description of his stint in Hollywood, hacking out screenplays à la Fitzgerald in the 1930's. He was living in a very thin-walled apartment complex next to a former humour writer for the New Yorker. He established this guy as such and added that he was frequently to be heard laughing bitterly, alone in his apartment. Then at several intervals when describing tense ~~scenes~~ or ridiculous melodramatic scenes in his apartment he would punctuate them with the spontaneous guffaws of the New Yorker guy. It was very, very funny. Oldies are crowding all the shady benches! Let's hear it for dehydration! Gimme a D! Hey! Roll that guy over and make him give me a goddamn D!

Too many old people in Cefalù. Very resorty. I have had my fill of horrible, horrible legs. I have seen veins I can't even describe to you. Some Germans behind me are talking about Auschwitz. Ach. OK. I get out of here, we'll see if you get any more out of me today. Nope, can't leave yet, just noticed I'm being cased by a giovanotto on the boardwalk. He looks like he gives good chase. Keep...walking... OK...finally clear.

15h30 and still no sign of the Dutch boy. There's got to be a better way to do this. I was just subjected to the loudest, most obnoxious cat-calling I've ever experienced and it lasted the length of an entire block. It will be interesting to see how things go now that I will be in male company. I wonder if I will be spared humiliating spectacles like that. I wanted to turn back and start throwing punches.

I am still dreading the reception I will get when I return to "the apartment". Remember that movie? What a great movie. Do you have a favourite movie? I don't know much about your taste in movies at all. Except that the last movies you saw in the theatre were "Old School" and "Anger Management". Not such a shit hot track record, son. There is something impeding my straw. Would it be coarse to blow it out, pea-shooter style? Maybe at the Aryan specimen headed toward me? Hey, it's like I willed him to take a seat across from me! Look at us, we're young, we're alone in a strange land, we're sitting across from one another. What happens next? I shoot a lemon seed at you and whatever will be will be? Mom. Such a fount of wisdom that one.

I'm telling you, my wrists are getting so burnt from writing to you. I can never seem to find a patch of shade for them. My left wrist: totally shaded right now. My right? Mercilessly exposed. I need a cabana boy to hold umbrellas over me wherever I go, like Puffy.

I'm gonna get that Dimme for making me waste a whole afternoon like this. Moronic. Pick a train and take it, dude! So if the letters drop off (you know, like start coming every <u>other</u> day instead of every day) a) you will be relieved, I know it. But b) it will be because my every moment is engaged in entertaining the puppyish yet suddenly labile Dutchman.

Next is time for the volcanoes. I was reading about them just now. Lotsa pumice and limestone and the like. I will take a boat out there in a few days. Dimme and I are going to Palermo and Monreale tomorrow. The great thing about him is he will follow my lead more than happily. Where have I heard that before, the "more than happily" part? Oh yes, it was you, but you were "so much more than happy". A slight bastardization. Then you quibbled with my theory of eternal happiness, which of course was absurd. Contrary to your burbling, the merits of my assertion are as sound as the shocks on your new "sports car". If you being a reliable presence on your end makes me happy, and your being just that in turn makes you "so much more than happy" then why shouldn't it follow that if I ask for no more than that then we will both be happy forever and ever, or at least until I get home from Italy? You can call me all the fancy pants, compound, doctor's son names you want, but don't piss on my logic. My logic will not be pissed on!

Cheap knick knacks all around me. Many people have requested gifts, isn't that gauche of them? "Bring me back something!" Hey, f you, buddy! I'll bring you back something if the spirit bloody well moves me to.

What time could it possibly be now? Can it really be only 4 minutes after when I started? No. It must have been 15h when I started.

I'm hoping I'll catch Dimme here on his way to meet me at the Duomo. Getting reeeeeally bored. No people to watch, as these are the napping hours. I'm really very opposed to this complete shut down between 1 and 4. Until a nice family invites me in to include me in whatever the fuck they do during this interval, I will remain so.

Ah B. What are ya doin' now? Sitting at work again you delinquent? Do you have to use Holiday days for these little chauffeuresque escapades? There hasn't been an unsunny day here yet. I think I'm going to be a tree when I get home. Too much sun, almost. Certainly my wrists think so.

So easy to fall into the rhythms of this sort of life. I feel my mind do the familiar unclenching, it's always so exciting. Lee wrote me a world class email, and at the bottom he signed off with "run hard, write well." In a way it's ~~tacky~~ goofy, a tropism? What is that word? But I also ~~thi~~ remember it every morning and every morning its effect is more galvanizing.

    I do my best, you know,
        Michelle

May 8/03

Dear B,

What I didn't understand in the email I read yesterday—which was a fine and jolting and bone-stirring way to end our day—was that part about being trapped in a work of art. You said that was what your 10 page letter, excuse me, MY 10 page letter, taught you. ~~Did~~ Are you saying your letter is a work of art? Did you forget me and write a letter to yourself instead? Write <u>me</u>. And I will beg, and I'm not too proud or embarrassed, but I am curious about just what this now defunct part of your letter was referring to. Of course I am. But the part about being trapped in art I did not understand. Did you write me a letter from David Byrne or Mary Anfinsen? Is that why? I want one from you.

I am sitting on my balcony, watching Dimme swim in the pool down below. It's stupidly fun. He has been granted an additional two days with me due to good behaviour. I was very glad to see him, although ultimately, if you can stretch your mind back to my last letter, he kept me waiting for 4 and a half hours. I was half mad with impatience near the end, and had to retrieve his cell phone # from my email, buy a new phone card since I realized I had left a full one <u>in</u> the last phone I used. Then I couldn't get the bum one the train guy sold me to work and I threw it to the ground in anger and saw that this was one of the rare phones that takes coins. Then I got ahold of Dimme and he told me he was 5 min from the train station. Later he informed me that I was wrong to throw away the card, I just wasn't using it correctly. It was different from the telecom ones I am generally sold. Then when we get back to the apartment nice guy Massimo charged me 15€ for breaking the washing machine door and I felt so bad. It was not a good day. The only good part was writing to you. But ultimately seeing Dimme is a joy, he is the same as ever. Massimo, however, was not quite as thrilled, and I could see my stock went down drastically with him.

Dimme is jealous of you because, apparently, it is obvious that I am completely preoccupied with you and he told me he could tell I was in trouble the second I said your name. I've always liked how affectionate he is, he loves to hug and kiss, usually whenever the notion hits him, and there's something guileless and lovely about it. I wish I were more like him in that respect because I have urges to throw my arms around people all the time but rarely indulge them.

Yesterday we went to Palermo and Monreale for the day. Taking the train back to Cefalù, I had one of those moments that break your heart a little bit. Sweet Dimme was dozing in the seat across from me, he brought his iPod, the first I've seen and he let me mess around with it. I saw that he had one Weezer song, "Island in the Sun" and I put it on. The window was open and the wind was swatting my hair around with schoolboy hands and I was looking at Dimme and the mountains and countryside. I've only had a few moments in my life where this happens and I feel ~~lik~~ them like a sneeze coming on—is it going to happen? Is it the real thing?—and can hardly recall them when they're done. [Wait—Dimme interlude, he's such a jerk. He just got out of the pool and is laughing and said he feels that we ~~w~~ are a 50 year old couple, me reading a romance novel—which I'm not! I swear!—Him relaxing from his boring job. Then he said "What are we having for dinner, hon?" and I said "I'm going to serve you your ass on a plate." Should I go down there and push him in the pool?]

So in these moments you become acutely aware of yourself, every hour that has passed before, your exact age (not that old!) and the perfection of this moment that is doomed to end and will never happen again and you'll look back on fondly until you die and Rivers Cuomo singing about never feeling bad anymore. So yeah, had one of those.

Palermo I didn't like, only the Palace Chapel, and Monreale's duomo made me very very still. I won't bother trying to describe them, maybe I should try to save some things to tell you about. Inevitably I can't tell you everything, but I tell you what I remember in the moment of writing this…last night I was thinking I should cut it out. Maybe that will pass. Tell me why it warms your heart when I don't like you, you weirdo. I like it when you tell me stuff like that though. I liked your VCR story too…what a pair of bleeding hearts we would have made eh? A game of monopoly would have ended in tears and the writing of an acrostic poem. My childhood sentimental (heavy on the mental) hijinx are well documented... ~~I~~ even before the garbage bag debacle there was my dad buying a new car. Oh I hated that, grand mal sobbing fits. All those fun rides in the green convertible! My childhood sitting in a junkyard! The humanity! I was 4 again! A few years later I had another attack when my mom handed down the dictum that our Christmas tree was only to have red and green lights that year, when previously they had always been multi-coloured. Total meltdown. Why was this happening to me? Why would she do that? I have so little to hang onto here with this family tradition racket! Don't take away the multi-coloured lights too!

On a side-note, Christmas and trees etc were flashpoints where my mom was concerned. In one instance, which even my dad looks back on with a shudder, I had taken it upon myself to decorate the tree, since no one else was doing it and my mom was living in Toronto during the week. I think I was 9 or 10. Anyway, I ~~am~~ was a perfectionist and took great pains as usual. When my mom got home from TO. She was wordlessly unimpressed with my handiwork and immediately began dismantling it, decorating it in what I can only describe as the

Department Store tradition, using knick knacks she had brought from the big, glamourous, mother-stealing city. My mom was at her worst at Christmas time. Dimme is gone now. I sent him away. And what of me today, B? The beach? Yesterday was so tiring. I think we both need to languor a bit. But you can never languor just a bit, can you. That wouldn't be languorous of you.

Your email...I miss you. I slept very badly. You don't miss me. You don't. It's so good to be here. It's not a vacation. It's the month of the year I get to live my life. Maybe some people don't even get that much. I will be damned if I get a month for the rest of my life! Sometimes I find myself so funny. Here being alive is an endless loop of smirks and eyes rounding and snapping and heart swelling, like yours did. It's so strange having Dimme here, it's like he just wandered into a dream I was having. A dream with no people, only animals, or talking appliances, or shuttered doors and mine too. He brought me crazy Dutch waffles. Haven't had one yet but they certainly look crazy. Maybe on the plane home I can convince myself briefly that it is the third consecutive flight I have taken and that all bets are off and shove one in my mouth before I smell a rat.

We are going to climb La Rocca, a huge hill with an ancient temple at the top, later today. Massimo wants us all to go to dinner tonight. He said "You can bring your <u>boyfriend</u>" the last word ~~eo~~ shooting from his mouth like a watermelon seed.

I'm sad I missed your water jug joke. I remembered I haven't told you my second favourite joke of all time yet. Remind me of that at an appropriate moment and I'll tell you. I love it. It's got all my favourite elements.

I'll go now, let you get back to not missing me. Tell me why you need me there. Tell me what you need from me. Tell me how to make it easier for you to tell me.

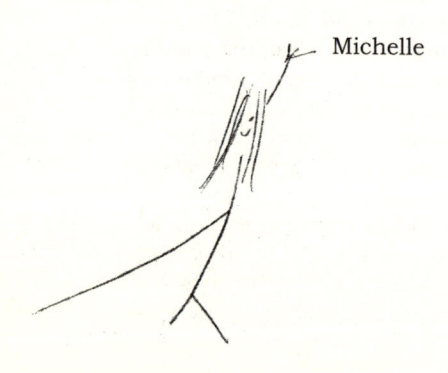

                        Michelle

May 9/03

Dear B,

One thing I noticed here that I keep forgetting to tell you is that most of the time when strangers approach me they address me in French. I don't know why I am suddenly assumed to be a Frenchie, since there are more Germans and Italians here, but the Sicilians always bust out whatever French they know in talking to me. Of course they can't tell how crappy my French is because theirs is even worse. Anyway. It just happened again so it struck me to finally tell you.

Woops, little bit of pencil smudgage up there. I see. I should have closed the book before shoving it in my bag. Oh so temperate here today. Not much sun. My hair and neck and wrists are safe you will perhaps be glad to know. Or maybe you've moved on to the shoulder, instep and earlobe and the former triumvirate is old hat. Ho hum. I just found the coolest little niche, down a staircase on the ~~mi~~ northwest side of the town. It's the labryrinth of lava rocks, like a peewee mountain range, many many hiding places and several straight up caves. The lava made thrones, settees, credenzas, armoires and a fainting couch or two for our resting pleasure. Hidden, or so I thought, from the human eye. I stretched out on a rock or two and thought about you, watching the water splash a few feet below. It was about 15 minutes before I heard the heart-sinking sound of wolf whistles above me. And I know my face wore an expression of sad resignation, much like that worn by Christ Pantocrator in the duomo, as I heard the shufflings and scramblings of 4 male feet tottering toward my back. But, I say B, it certainly was nice while it lasted. I will take you there, that's where I would take you.

As I was grudgingly packing myself up to jump and weave my way off the rocks, I knew I was in for a chase, and indeed, I only lost them by stepping into a posh jewellrey store. Ever the opportunist, I took my unforeseen arrival in such a store as a sign that I should finally buy that watch I've been talking about. The whole thing took about 5 minutes. ~~B~~ I always buy the first one I see and never look back. It usually works. Oh I hate shopping. But I did insist he fashion me one of those band-holders to keep the band from flapping around. There's a lot of band to hold down, as I have to fasten the watch on the last notch. You know, sunsore, withered wrists and all.

Now I am on a bench with two old men. I think they are arguing about my insolence in sitting down on their bench. I could snap them both like breadsticks. I love it here. Not here, Cefalù, the town itself is not my favourite, just here. I love being with Dimme, we have done very well. He made me laugh yesterday while descending the Rocca. At the halfway point there are the ruins of what seems to be an ancient household. We crawled all over them and Dimme started mapping out our imaginary house (he was absolutely ecstatic with yesterday's trek, couldn't stop loving it). He said, "this would be the kitchen, this would be a patio, and here's the bedroom, where I would bring you breakfast in bed every morning: 'Here you go, honey!'" and he mimed cracking open a can of pop. Yes, I shoved him into a pillar, but I was laughing. And sure enough this morning while I was running he went out and bought me a six pack of pop.

He lets me listen to his iPod while I run, and I've just got to get one. He is hot into competition with you over memory. He says there's a 30 gig one now. He sent me out the door with the ipod with the warning that if I broke it I had to buy him a new one and it had to be bigger than yours. I didn't break it.

~~Th~~ But I listened to Katrina and the Waves over and over. There is a group of kids, all in blue baseball hats demolishing ice cream cones behind me...they are playing this game where they dare each other to walk by me and say "hell-o" and then run ecstatic back to their group. It seems to amuse them exceedingly. They looked at the letter I am writing and cleverly deduced that I speak English, so "hell-o" it was. They were actually pushing this one little guy toward me, he whining and protesting "Noooo-o," that's when I caught on and I turned and saw his little face smiling, bashful and miserable. Who knew "hell-o" was so exotic?

I think we will see an Italian movie tonight—well actually, I think it will be a dubbed American one—they have turned

"Van Wilder" into a Tara Reid movie called "Maiae College". The Van Wilder guy isn't even on the poster! How did that happen? I guess we'll see. God, I may even have to see the original when I get home. The sacrifices I make. Completist.

And have you seen any movies? Rented? I agree with your seeing and watching distinction by the way. Bravo. I am now reading a book called "The Last Samurai". So far I hate it. I should have known better than to trust the recommender. It's weird that our translations of Bovary differ on melting/moving the stars. It would be exceptionally difficult to melt a star, it being a ball of fire and all, therefore I like my version better. I have a feeling old guy #2, Mrs. Grey Cardigan, is going to ~~start~~ give me a brown cane beat down any second so I'm going to sign off and send this.

> What *is* that woman eating?
> Michelle

May 10/03

Dear B,

And how! Yes, so true! No, not at all, you doorknob. I am responding to your letter, which Massimo handed to me yesterday. He yelled for me to come down, seemed to be in a big hurry, and I came running. When I snatched it from his hands I turned and began skipping back towards the stairs. I noticed a guest of our British neighbours eyeing me bemusedly. Funny that the night before, Friday, I despaired of receiving the letter and when I heard Massimo come in late to his office I went and stood on the balcony trying to send beams of will-bending to the office down below. Dimme laughed at me. I stood there for a long time.

I liked the comic strip and the "l&". I like it when you write my name too. I read the letter over and over. I am in the port in Milazzo, waiting for the boat to Lipari. I just said good-bye to Dimme on the train, who is continuing on to Catania. I seem to get cranky whenever I see a computer now, which may in part explain my impatient emails. It was funny to see Dimme, who had this cell phone which he checked constantly for "text messages" and used to call people all the time and who would want to go to the computer place all the time. Bad influence on me because then I would start using the damn computer too. He's different from me in that he needed constant contact with home and talked of all the people he missed. I don't miss anyone. I mean—I miss you, the you I know, but I don't miss my life in Toronto. At all. Dimme missed his life a whole lot and he's only been here 2 weeks. That's probably a good thing, right? Just a different approach to a vacation maybe. I try to totally cave it. I wonder when we will see each other again.

Oh the old men have got my back today, boy. I love them. I love the bloody old men. So now I go back under the radar with Dimme's bad influence gone. If I could just figure out when this ticket office opens I'd be all set.

Why did you get so mad at me on Friday, B? Don't you know that that is worse than insolent, it's pointless? But you should tell me, I'm interested in why. Is it because you think I am evil and you're good? Is it because I'm not absurdly beautiful? I'm sorry. I wish I were. My face is covered in freckles now. It's retarded. Freckle city and my back is once again peeling. It's disconcerting to see how the body remembers the past harms you have done to it. I am peeling around the same perimetre as last year's burn. Scary. I think I am defiled. Is it because I have a new watch and you do not? What is with this new Madonna song? It's <u>horrible</u>. It's 'or-eeee-bluh! That rap shit? And I saw the cheesiest video for it on TV in this little tavola calda place. What is she thinking?

I am interested to hear about your new writing. How is it going? Are you back at your home now? I am feeling good today, always look forward to the new place. We went to see that "Maial College" last night. God that was (unintentionally) funny. Something about dubbing is always a surefire shortcut to laffs. Why do I always hear 'Messina' as 'Messinia' in my head? Can't seem to get it straight. Mr. Fixative It. You are.

I am sorry for your colleague whose marriage imploded. That was a very sad story. I think I need to go check on the ticket office action. Hang on lievie.

OK. So that went fairly well. No casualties. I am on the boat waiting to pull out to sea. Wheeeee! I like boats. Whoopeee. Hydrofoils are fun because they go so fast! This sucker would leave your parents' whatever etc. you called it in the…mist. Tried to think of an aquatic equivalent to dust. Results mixed.

It's beautiful again, as predicted. Dimme chagrinned. I should say though that yesterday was also lovely. I spent the laziest day yet. Shuffling around, drinking pop, scribbling. Went down to the pool, lazed, read. Such a beautiful breeze weaving through the mountains. I felt, dare I say it, lucky. Ha ha, I see an ad on the back of one of these boat seats for "Radio Kiss Kiss," my favourite station from last year. Loved Radio Kiss Kiss. Some ad, though. Doesn't even give you the call numbers. Those forgetful Italians. They mean well. To compliment our night of cheesy Italotainment I permitted Dimme to ignite the little TV we had. There was this intriguing, inscrutable variety show-cum-competition on one channel, and we couldn't stop watching. Freaks from all over Europe came to ~~pro~~ put their freakdom on display for Italy. Dimme even recognized the Dutch offering, calling him "the Michael Bolton of illusionists" with such rue that I laughed to excess. He said watching TV with me was like watching it with one of his boy friends. I wasn't sure how to take that. There was this French acrobat woman named, improbably, "Aurelia Cat". She was doing things with her body I did not believe possible, or believed certainly as improbable as the name "Aurelia Cat". It's hard to describe my conclusion about spending time in Italy with someone else. It instantly changes the tenor of things. As you could see, I was suddenly doing very "vacationy" things like lying by a pool and checking my email twice a day. It might fly for a few days, but my time here has always been so far removed from that. Part of me was itching to reclaim that.

E alora, eccomi. I was thrilled beyond all dignity when my cab driver (it was too far from the stazione to the port, sadly) told me my Italian was *not bad at all. I was going to put that in quotes but then I remembered he said it in Italian.

My hair is turning the most bizarre colour. I don't think the chlorine helped. Hoo, the sun is beating through this window. Let's get this show on the road! Andiamo, smoking men. Please take me to Lipari adesso. Hm! It's like they read English. And so we go. I love this language. Dimme's curiosity is boundless. He made friends with all of our neighbours and was hurt by the coolness of the German bitches next door to his neighbourly overtures. It is his first time to Italy (!) and already he has a good basic command. Well, OK, semi-basic. But it was the lengths he went to...he has always been a very avid student of English, constantly asking me for the most accurate words for complicated things ("serendipity" and "complacent" are the 2 he got out of me this morning) and he bought a picture book intended to teach Italian children English to get his start. I really admire his facility with language. When I hear him talk on the phone I always get a little shock. Dutch is a crazy language. Very hard for me to get my tongue around. Dimme says it's impossible for anyone over 25 to learn Dutch and speak it without an accent. I believe him.

"The Last Samurai", the book I am reading, deals in large part with languages. Funny that "Earthly Powers" did too, so the phe-

nomenon of my reading materials engaging
one another in dialogue continues. This one
is about a child prodigy who begins learn-
ing all sorts of languages very early. It's not
a good book. I wish I were reading a classic.
I should have brought another classic.
What will Lipari be like? The water is all a-
sparkle. Bodies of water. So fearsome. I see
another boat in the distance, big one.
Hmmmmmmm. Sleepy now. Do you miss
me? Are you awake yet on a Sunday morning? I don't know many of the singers you
mention, so I may make mistakes ~~strai~~ of
omission, or non-omission similar to those
of the you-know-what girl at the jukebox.
I'd know friggin' "Surrender" though. Jesus.
I already wanna cap that "Shit, Man" guy's
teeth. Is that an expression? I think it
should be. Violence for pansies. If I move to
NYC I won't be hanging out in those bars.
They'll make my heart ache. Give me a bar
with illiterate old men over so haute and
sharp any and every friggin' day of the
week. And twice on Sunday. That's one of
my alternate band names. We have the
Confabulations (is that taken?) one I can't
recall this second and Twice on Sunday.
But Miss Torso still in the lead.

I am attempting to read the Italian paper
jammed between the seats. The "Gazzetta
del Sud". Ooh, it's today's! Soccer scores

above all else. Bad shit going down in
Napoli. Nasty Napoli.

Whoa! Big island incoming! Vulcano? OK B,
I end this here before I get seasick and
ralph all over my brown brown ankles.

    Ci vediamo dopo, you know,

        Michelle

Dear B,

Today I am tired of writing to you. Perhaps it was bound to happen and, as you would say, perhaps not. I am lying on one of Vulcano's black beaches, the ones you already seem to know about, and wondering if there's anything I can tell you that you don't already know. I know you're curious or whatever and obsessed with amassing information, but occasionally this irritates me, as it leaves me, as I mentioned, with the unsavory feeling that you are determined to stay one step ahead of me, even where my own experiences are concerned. I feel now that I will have nothing to tell you, which is odd because we all agree that you know nothing. Oh great who's this dicksqueeze who just sat down beside me? Fucking Christ this gets old.

And I mean <u>right</u> fucking beside me. On a huge deserted stretch of beach. Black beach. Remember? Of course you do, you know all about them. I don't know exactly why but your email put me in a foul mood. And this buttmunch isn't helping. Maybe I should leave this alone until I feel better. Fucking asshole, I hate this fucking guy. He's looking at me like he's waiting for me to pop out of my bikini or something. I want to hurt him, stupid ignorant rude motherfucker. I hate you you fat, ridiculous cocksucking piece of shit.

It's much later and he finally left, after much continued profanity on my part. The things I was thinking! Anyway, back to the other, I think the main thing is I consider it no fun at all to tell a person about something spectacular when that person has already read about it on the internet and believes they already know all about it. In other words, it's no fun for it to go something like this: "So tell me about the black beaches!" "Tell me about the Neapolis." "Tell me about the mud baths." "Tell me about the temple of Zeus." "Tell me about the piazza marconi in Agrigento where, at 1 pm, the boys parade around on their

Vespas like bees circling the hive." And I'd say "Wait a minute, how could you possibly know about that you knobgobbler?" It's not that I feel thunder being stolen, because that's not possible. I'm here, and there's no comparison between exposure to facts and experience, it's just fun being taken out of it for me. Sometimes Lee does that, mainly with music and movies and books. Is that enough of my complaining? I just don't want you to wonder why I'm not regaling you with stories when I come home. I have a feeling it will be no fun. Your curiosity is one of the things I like about you but you take it too far sometimes. Like, maybe I am the foray into knowledge about Canadians. I am the thing that will allow you to say "Oh yes, Canadians are like this" or "Canadian girls like this or that." Am I that? Would you say stuff like that? Like getting out your Mme Bovary and fact-checking the passage I wrote out for you? What's that all about? You are funny. But with Lee, it's the tendency that annoys me most about him. Could I be projecting? I don't think so smarty, though I assume that's what your prognosis will be. You know you do this, I've heard you lament it to me.

Enough.

I am afraid to go in the water because I have seen these gelatinous creatures in the damp upper lip between the water and the sandy sand. I think they must be jellyfish. Those bite, right? I've never seen one before! I do wish you could see what I see. It's a beautiful u-shaped beach with grey mountains pitching up on every side like rocket exhaust. The air is whispery and kind of sweet here. There seems to be a different quality to the air on every beach. You mentioned in your letter going to museums in Spain. Certainly I would like this, the Prado is on the big list. Got to see that Bosch. I am now reading McCarthy on Venice. If you think I'm cranky you should check _her_ out. She says Lawrence loved Italy and I would quote you what he wrote about it à propos of your musing on how if he wrote about Italians they would all be naked but now I don't feel like it. It might set off another round of fact-checking. Damn you and your fact-checking! After this I am out of books. That wasn't supposed to happen. God this letter is boring. It is very hard to think on the beach. Vuul-caa-no. It's always giggle-worthy to me when I hear an actual German say "Wunderbar!" or Italian "Maronne!" or French "Sacre bleu!" You wonder who let central casting work your vacation. It is confirmed that I will shortly be poor as a

Church mouse. Black black sand...it looks so incredible matted to your feet or the inside of your arm when you turn over. Can't believe I forgot my damn camera. There's a stretch of tall grass before me that looks like the one bordering the ball-field in Field of Dreams. It seems to be on a crest of some sort. I see a row of grass and then sky. For all I know oblivion could be on the other side. Or: a tennis court! Man this sand is crazy. I'd really like a picture of it clinging in some mappish coastline on my arm. It's too damn cool.

Chubby lovahs beside me can't get enough of the water. Don't they know it's full of cree-tures? I walked around the island before coming here. It's lovely, lots of farms set between the mountains, streets as narrow as a Radio Flyer. I ♥ this coffee grind beach.

Am I ungrateful and terrible? Maybe.

I just spoke with my dad on the phone after about a week and a half. He mentioned that he had just read parts 4 + 5 (Basta Cosi) I was kind of dreading this, but he said he really liked them and I tried to change the subject anyway. His stock went up though. I'm glad he could appreciate them for what they are, whatever that may be. Man, where I am now there is a really powerful sulphur smell—still on Vulcano. No way am I taking a roll (splat? tumble? squish?) in that stinky thermal mud. I don't consider mud all that theraputic.

So the first people on these islands was 5000 BC.?! Looking at them, Cefalù and others too but especially these islands, you really have to marvel at human endeavour. How the fuck did they find them? Why did they colonize? Did they fear nothing? When I think of people I know who have never even left Canada, and all the places I am still afraid of or uninterested in going to, I can't believe the drive of the Greeks and earlier civilizations to strike out. It's kind of a shame we've discovered every inhabitable surface of this world. Imagine how exciting it must have been to them to be alive on this strange, limitless planet. Maybe they would have been disappointed to know that it didn't get any better than this. That reminds me, in the exquisite Monreale duomo, Dimme said "It must have been an amazing thing to be a true believer back then" meaning how lucky to be a Christian and have such a monument to your belief to stoke its fervour. I wondered, though, if that were true. Often I have thought the same thing...but...ah, let's save it for a conversation. Religion is tough. Ha ha. Boy I'm on fire today, eh? That was an epigram worthy of Goethe.

Really I dream about whether those settlers were too busy for the petty occupations that keep us going now. Glances, dancing alone, eating apples. It's hard for me to connect with them in that way, no matter how many wine glasses, painted vases and amphitheatres I see. That they cried and, oh god, laughed and all that shit that is making me sound like a heel. That they looked just like we do. When I see that little fishbone ~~mus~~ splay of muscles that connects a man's pectoral to the abdominal— you know that little ~~iso~~ scalene patch on either side?—on Greek statuary it always fells me. 'My God! They had *that* too?' ~~It~~ The human body, so unchanged in thousands of years. Is it the same for the mind? I fear for our times. Ah. I do. I don't care, I do. Technology is out of control, it's preying on fundamental human weaknesses which should be beaten out like dust in a rug. Vicious circle of paranoia, insecurity and alienation fed by increasingly manifold avenues of checking, cross-checking, hip-checking, cheque-bouncing. Too many options for feeding the beast. Maybe every generation has feared this but that doesn't mean there's ever been a greater reason than now. Sometimes I feel so uneducated. So ignorant. Do you wish for a mentor? I do. What else do you wish for? Non voglio più...

Guy just walked by while I was writing and said "Inglese?" and I said "Si." without looking up or stopping what I was doing. That felt pretty cool. He kept going and I kept going. Oh sun. The wrists are mighty sore today, my pet. What will you ever do in the way of reparations? Dance the tarantella?

REPARATION'S 1 TRUE LOVE ← REPARATIONS "Let me by you dancing monkey!"

Whoa!! I almost literally missed the boat there, I was so engrossed in my artwork. I just ran down to the pier and jumped on as it was pulling out

I, like you, was a better artist as a child.

Wheeeee! Hydrofoilin'! I'm in the basement of the boat where all the froth happens. I'm in the thick of it now, pop tart! I feel happy. As Katrina would say, "I feel alive, I feel the love, I feel my love and it's really real!" Were more perfect lyrics ever written, or sung?

Nick Hornby's blight of a canonization aside, that really is a perfect pop song. I never, ever tire of it.

What's with you and gospel music? Did you forget you're an old Jew or what? Remember Elvis doing gospel in the '68 Comeback special? I love that "I'm Saved" song. The black guys in full-body leotards leaping and writhing around. It's all very kinky, as it should be. Which begs the question of my hormonal situation, as does most everything, if you put your mind to it. Begs indeed.

> Begging off,
>
> Michelle
> (1*le*)

May 12/03

Dear B,

I have a bad feeling about a series of letters I sent you. It occurs to me, upon consulting my little log, that there seems to be some sort of pothole ~~the~~ in the works. You have not received, I am assuming from your email, a letter since May 7, this corresponds with my purchase of new stamps, which I assumed were still good but am now wondering if I made a mistake. I think they were a few cents less per stamp. Now I am paranoid that at best it is going to take twice as long for those to get to you and at worst someone at Poste Italia is going to say "Che brutta!" and throw them away, as there is obviously no return address they can get to. This would mean, maybe about

7 letters going AWOL. That would suck. In any case, I am dearly hoping they recommence their shuffling off to Manhattan. I'd even settle for Buffalo, at least it's still NY.

I read your email, yes I got your letter! Duh. That's what my email reference to "absurdly beautiful" was all about. I even put it in quotes to refresh your memory. Who did you think I was quoting? Neruda? Even he would have picked up on that and he's dead! I am sitting at my apartment waiting for my towel and bikini to dry so I can head to Canneto. Of course after my machine-molesting exploits in Cefalù I was understandably gunshy when I saw the washing thing, but my running clothes, should they get the notion, would have little trouble catching a boat to Stromboli without me at this point and fear won over reason. Of course I couldn't get it to work so I put the clothes in a pile in my room, spilled detergent on top of them. I was touched to see, when I returned from running that someone had spirited my sweaty stash away, presumably to the machine, though I was somewhat less thrilled to find, when I returned from a romp around town, that my underpants ad etceteratum were waving around in the apartment courtyard. The underpants, however, looked pleased as punch about the development. I'll save the story of how I ended up where I am for a conversation, it's funny, and involves a hustler grandma type. Needless to say I'm going to be so broke when I get home I can barely stand to think about it.

As for staying at Bingo's place, I'm all for it! But if he's back at the end of May, we're kind of screwed. If he should ever go away for a stretch of time in the future, however, you tell him I'd be more than happy to check his faxes, voice mail, stork deliveries and skywriting by word of mouth. I regret, however, that I cannot tend to any plant life he may have. I'm from Canada, we don't have those there. Plaid thumbs, all of us.

Have you read The Iliad? Why didn't I bring it for this trip? Me so stupid! It would have been perfect. Ah letters. I like getting them. Do you? I slept unbelievably hard last night, I had no idea where I was when I woke up. "Where the fuck am I?" I'm still not sure. Ask me to tell you about the funny thing that Dimme did that made me helpless with laughter. It made me love him so much.

Oh happy little island. You make me sweat so much! The padrone di casa loves to garden and he sings while he does it. I love that. How weird that you emailed me about band names when just yesterday I wrote you about same. I'm telling you, it happens all the time. You and your stupid psychic powers. I'm not sure I recall which time you are referring to about talking on the phone. But I like talking to you. Last night I was wishing I could talk to you for a little while. Your day sounded nice. I liked the part about "then I took everyone out to dinner." Do they ever take you out? I picture this cute little group in a cute little restaurant where cute people go and people like me walk by and glance in the window thinking about hollowed out watermelons. What kind of impression do you think you make when you're all out and about like that? Do you relish it? You asked me if I knew something you didn't about being in it for keeps. The answer is no. I think you know it too.

And so, what else do I have to tell you today? Book continues to suck. Yet I will persevere. Your story about Marcel and his idiotique grasp of American idioms was great. That Marcel. What a postcard he is. So you are done with him? Is he still looking to overpay someone to edit and update his web site? Because I am still willing to be overpaid. I was on the wall about it for a while but when the cheezies are down, you have to go for the appetite.

I was Ms. E. Lusive in your last dream, huh? What's that all about? My mom arrived in Florence yesterday. It seems we will meet in Rome. This means Toronto homeward bound date is now the 26th.

Do you think the Aeolian sun has made quick work of my damp vestments? I think I'll go find out.

     Best anyway, dreamer,
         l*e*

Su, dai!

May 14/03

Dear B,

I've got to stop writing you email! It's bad for both of us. Plus it occurred to me that it's rather silly for me to be writing you email to check if my real letter has arrived yet. Last night I came the closest I ever have to wanting to hurt a child. There was this boy outside my window while I was trying rather desperately to concentrate on something. He had this thing, I think it ~~mo~~ was a dog's chew toy, it made the most grating wheeze-squeak when deployed/squeezed and he would not stop. There was every variation of wheeze-squeak and he was determined to suss them all out. It was so loud. I couldn't believe ~~she~~ Rosa didn't come out to holler at him like she does the dogs when they begin their desperate barking. Do you find barking dogs upsetting? I do. They seem absolutely <u>beside</u> themselves...it makes me wonder what could be so wrong.

It has been 3 days and Rosa still hasn't asked me for money. Then again she's got my passport so she knows I'm not going anywhere. I hate that custom of taking your passport. It's my passport! I'm very possessive of it! Dimme got me accustomed to smoking a cigarette in the evening so I actually bought myself a pack. The matches I got with them are so cute, wait til you see them—

Of course you probably know by now that I am lying about staying in Italy an extra week. That I will be in New York on the 23rd until the 26th. It seemed like more fun to surprise you. But of course I will be there. You said you needed me there, so that's where I'll be. It's getting scary though! I have a feeling you'll be sick of me, or at least fed up with me. I'll have to come up with a song and dance number to distract you from your disillusion with my apparent capriciousness. It's all misunderstanding. It's all distorted, things get lost in the transatlantication.

You asked me a few days ago, in ~~my~~ response to my story of the day of the magical bust-enhancing T-shirt, if you would have had the same reaction as the Italian men, what you would have thought. Honestly, I think no. I think the standards here are a lot lower, and besides that I am fully expecting to disappoint you in every conceivable way. And that, my friend, is my Waterloo of confessions.

Dear much-later-in-the-day-B. It is actually too bloody hot for me to be outside. I didn't think it possible but there you go. I spent the morning running, singing, shopping—I seem to have a lot of shopping to do—I have been looking for the best Italian fishing tackle for you...still not satisfied. But I did some decent work for a few other people on the list. I love singing. Sometimes at night when I know it's time for me to crack a notebook and put some work into something I procrastinate by singing and before I know it it's 2 hours later and I can't keep my eyes open. Wouldn't it be nice to make a living that way? Two years ago when I got back from Rome I was still so heartbroken and I was very serious about the idea of finding an accompanist and a shitty hotel bar that wanted a singer so I could have an outlet and sing heartbroken songs to lonely people every night. I'd sing "Lush Life" over and over. I know you question Linda Rondstat's big band period but the fact is that's the only album of hers I own. And I LOVE it.

Now I am going to walk to Canneto again, but this time I'm going to the white beaches of the Pumice quarry and caves. Black yesterday, white today. What a spectacular and varied life I am leading. I'm very very happy here. I never want to leave. I may never get the scampis again.

The men here seem very concerned about my being on foot. I am offered a ride every few minutes: "Passagio?" They can't believe it when I say no. One has been casing me for a few days, wanted to give me a lift when I was burdened with 6 2L water bottles. Today he finally asked my name and to go for a pizza. He rides alongside me while I walk, this time all the way to my destination—about 1 km—Villa Rosa. He is Fabrizio. Later as I passed—I mean, he's nice, seems like a swell guy—I swear I heard the familiar hissing and sucking sounds men make at women. I froze up and thought "Oh no, Fabrizio, don't break my heart. Et tu?" I'm not positive, but I really hope it wasn't him.

OK. Now I go for my epic walk up the coast

of the island. Walk walk walk. Oy vey. Oh, but thank you for sending the whole poem. I remembered the proper lines last night in bed...can't believe I got "dozen" wrong. And "went"...did you know I am taking an overnight ferry to Napoli? I am going to buy a dozen of each in Edna's honour before I get on. Maybe I will even give them away to someone's mother when I get there.

Dear B again...now I am on that beach, after one hell of a walk. Up and down and up and down and then all around and then one more time up and down. It does not appear to be white at all, in fact, until you're flat out on it and then the sun turns it into this reflective sheet of crystal. Blinding, glowing white. Very strange. Once again my excessive happiness was curtailed by the arrival of yet another short, fat, glasses-wearing ogler. I was so happy before though! I even made up a word: "eruptophilic", that is my description for Stromboli which I can at last make out on the horizon. Before it was hidden from me by Mon Rosa. The couple about a hundred feet from me seemed mere moments from having sex but it appears they are turning back from the breach. On the beach. That's the name of my first novel, did I tell you? The Breach on the Beach? This is the land of topless ladies. This is a beach of pumice, that's why it's so white, and while lying on my back I ground my heels into the rocks and sand and it felt so fucking good I was sure I was doing something wrong. As the sun is setting the air gets clearer and I have an even better view of the eruptophile. Pretty volcano. I booked a trip there this morning. Just found the strangest stone, it looks like one of those iced Peak Frean's cookies but it is exactly the shape of Sicily. I will give it to you. I feel like I have a million things to tell you. I'll never say it all. I was very happy just now, before the man, when I could laugh in topless peace. Now I must be silent, no more chattering. It makes me sad. The other day, on some other beach I saw a girl who made my heart ache a bit. Her body was so lovely, when she took off her clothes ~~her~~ she looked like she'd been dipped in a caramel milkshake. No, it defies my meager powers of description. She was small but perfectly shaped, she just looked smooth all over. I was very ashamed of my envy. I don't envy, generally. Sure I can get jealous if you, or anybody else, frankly, tells me about how "absurdly beautiful" a girl is (which is, in my opinion, very bad form) but I rarely envy another. But something about the lines of this girl's body made me think "If ~~had h~~ I had that body I wouldn't have a care in the world."

She was not beautiful, but her skin was truly marvelous. I wondered how her boyfriend could lie there beside her with such imperial disaffection when it was obvious that hands belonged on that body at all times. Hours later I was back in town and they walked right by me, looking infinitely less glamourous, she nothing special in her leggings and T-shirt. It made me shake my head in wonder. Shakey shakey.

Four-eyes finally packing it in. Bye, afternoon-ruiner! Silencer! Half-assed swimmer! Go whole-assed or go home! Last year in Tropea I remember being on a tear and writing something about having no other home and no other master than my notebook. It all got very dramatic, I was very perplexed...I was trying to figure out just where I was going to fit. Why should I choose this? Why will this fulfill me? The fact that I had no home seemed as good an answer as any.

Just beyond this beach is a place called "Acqua Calda" where the water will burn you if you are not careful. I will go, and walk and walk again. I'd like to take an Italian cat home. Would John like to add some foreign blood to his brood? In Rome I had a kind of epiphanic encounter with a cat on the Appia Antica. That was one of the greatest days of my life. I can see that damn volcano, B, it's smoking like the strumpet it is.

Goddammit I'm going to go there. I'm going to go there and everything's going to be OK.

> air @ Spiagge Bianche= mild with a slight snap of static cling

> Dear, dear B,
>
> Michelle

May 14/03

Dr Shcking Wrm,

I mean it B, the thought of those letters being FUBAR makes me want to hurl myself into a volcano. And it's not like I'm lacking for opportunity. Like I said (what feels like) a million years ago, writing to you was my answer to a journal. It was so much more fun telling you than telling a book. It's not like I wrote you a masterpiece every day or anything, still, it's 50 pages of things I saw and did, often while I was seeing and doing them, and I'll never be able to recall them all. Details, I like giving you details. Plus, I got to write things to you I'm not sure I'd have the nerve to say to your face. Ha. It's funny, I can travel, organize flights and apartments and ~~era~~ navigate craziness and orchestrate my own nirvana but when it comes to feeding myself or posting a letter I get tripped up. Ah. Got to stop thinking about the 50 pages. Gotta have faith they'll turn up eventually. Makes me want to get on a boat, then get on a train (my I'm inaccessible at the moment) and go back to that piazza in Siracusa and lower the boom. I will try to remember some of the bigger things that happened...oh that reminds me, in addition to screwing

Oh hell. The light I was writing by burned out at that exact moment. Who doesn't want me to write to you??

Oh yeah, Italian Post, no fucking in between, either 3 days or 3 months. So typical. So, being the completist that I am, I am now getting it both ways from Poste Italiane...tonight I sent a letter to you blowing my cover about coming to NYC, thinking it would not get there until after the 23rd. Then I see you got a letter in less than a week! Why why why!

Aaaieee! I despair I despair. I am lying in my bed, as I have lain (?) in several other beds writing to you. It's almost like talking to you at this point. Have I told you how much I like your voice? I like it a lot. I could point out for you the exact moments when I have liked it the most. If you fancy. You frustrate me. Your non-answers. "Okay." That's not an answer to a pointed question, put-er off—I just wanted to call you a putter offer but then it turned out my hybrids were each words in their own right. What happens then? I have taken us right through the facile labelling looking glass. The boy was out with his squeak toy tonight. To avoid the impending violence in my heart I took a walk into town. Plus: apples! Beautiful Lipari. Crazy country. It's true dammit everything functions but nothing works. Some paragon of modern thought made that point*, I think. Post office, shower, road, phone, visa machine, door, washing machine. I could go on all day. Did my letter tell you about how I broke the washing machine? See, these are things you really need to know. Did I confess yet about how I stiffed that dreaded Scampi waiter? Oh my, you should hear Rosa's voice...like scotch poured down sandpaper. Good scotch though. She's hollerin' tonight, boy! A little like the woman on the bus from Siracusa to Agrigento. Remember her? God I hope so.

Earlier today while buying peaches I got the most arresting smile from the woman

---

See Michelle use "point" 3 different way wout even meaning to! This is exactly the kind of thing you're missing! 7 letters worth! Can you stand it?

* Oh my God, a 4th! They said it couldn't be done!

out in front of the stall. It was when I was leaving. Another woman took my money, but I turned to exogreet (what's the word for the reverse greeting you do here that's not really good-bye but more like...an exo-greeting?) (We don't do it in Canada) and she was waiting expectantly for me to do just that, with this huge, goofy-toothed smile and even a little hand wave, which is <u>never</u> done. She made me happy. Like the Vietnamese guy in Toronto.

Again I wonder why I find it so imperative to take care of/with myself here. Maybe easy is a better word. At home it doesn't seem to matter as much, or at all. I'm really very reckless. I puzzle and puzzle over it. I wish I cared more for myself...it seems to be the thing to do. No one else will and all that. I just can't crack it. I come back here and I try and every time I think it's going to be different when I get home, that I've found the key, and every year I fail and resolve to come back to Italy...for longer. 1999-9 days, 2001-14 days, 2002-24 days, 2003- 30 days. I remember thinking in 2001, if this is what ~~20~~ 14 days does, what would happen to me after 3 months? ~~Th~~ So rarely do you see or fail to see, I should say, limits. Somewhat improbably, the contradictions everywhere slip perfectly, like intertwined fingers, into my corollary contradictions. I used to see the societal shut down between 1 and 4 as ridiculous and quaint, now I see 9-5 as barbaric and faithless. It makes perfect sense that you would work from 9-1, then stop, just as you are itching to, and go remember that you're a human being for a while. Then return for some leisurely hours of work which are mainly spent confabulating with passersby or dealing with orders of business in a manner befitting someone who knows the sunset is just around the corner. Literally and figuratively. ~~I o~~ While I was looking for fishing tackle for you today I wandered into one of the many tackle stores. A man greeted me heartily. I tried to get into it but he said "You speak English?" I said yes and he waved a very blonde, ethereal-looking woman over. She said "Can I help you" in a strange accent, maybe Nordic, but later resumed fluent (i.e. vehement) Italian with the man. I concluded that they must be married, running the show together, though she looked much younger and was very beautiful. I thought 'what the hell are you doing here?' Then children ran into the place, chasing around her and she scolded them accordingly. They were the strangest mix of this swarthy, squat, crinkly Italian fisherman and the willowy, ice blonde Botticelli girl. I thought "You

> I did not see what I was trying to say through to its conclusion. This is because I am eminently distractable. I should not read through my letters b/f sending.

did it, didn't you? You fucking did it." I'll wonder about that girl for a long time. So funny to hear this little Lord Fauntleroy-looking brat sounding off in Italian. So great.

Mmmm. I feel nice. Come over. We're both human beings, I'm sure it'll go off without a hitch.

May 15/03

Dear Sense,

I am at the base of Stromboli and it really is out of this world. The ride here was kind of nauseating, such choppy water. But I am in love with all 3 shipmen, and that helps. They dropped us here like bioinvaders and left us to scatter among the craters, scale the lava ripples, languish on the black sand. It's even blacker here than on Vulcano, and although it's quite overcast and windy...(the smoke from the volcano blots out the sun) the sand is warm like an electric blanket. Usually you dig your toes or your hands through the scorched crust to get to the cooler sand below, but here the deeper you go the hotter the sand. It's extremely unnerving and utterly fucking fantastic. I stretched out there for a long time, all alone on the huge beach, looking up at the smoking Stromboli. Coming around the effacement that is completely a sheet of lava I couldn't believe it was happening. You might ask yourself what kinds of people might choose to live at the base of an eruptophile. Well now I can tell you. A very singular people. Strange looking, island inbreeding narrowness about the eyes. They are the men running water forgot. I went up the one bar here to get a pop and had to run a gauntlet of wild-haired, dirty-faced men on ~~a~~ the stoop. I turned into the bar and immediately saw the bartender behind the bar, practicing medieval dentistry on some poor bastard, wrenching at something in his mouth with a pair of plyers. I think I casually turned on my heel and began the descent, but I can't remember exactly. I didn't order, I know that. The sun is setting. One more hour before we get back on the boat to circle around and see the rivers of fire. While waiting to leave in Lipari I was approached by a boy I have seen several times. Each time he tries to sell me a tour package. He looks kind of like an Italian Jude Law. This time he sat and talked with me for over an hour while I waited. His English is good, he spent 5 years in the States, I guess. He's going to meet me when I get off the boat at home. Unless I run off with the skipper.

Oh B, it's all so overwhelming. You have to promise to come here some day. It really is the queerest place. It feels haunted and all too alive at once. Bartolo, the boy, told me that last December a huge chunk of the volcano dropped off into the ocean, causing a 20 metre breaker and wiping out roads, houses, etc. He said in Lipari the water level suddenly rose noticeably and everyone started freaking out, wondering what was going on, just as all their cell phones began to ring with panicked Strombolians on the other end. They all had to move to Lipari for 2 months. I just saw where the chunk fell off. Incredible. Many kids from surrounding islands go to school on Lipari, they take a boat instead of a bus to school. If the water is choppy: "Sorry! No school!" Isn't that awesome? I tried to explain the Canadian parallel of snow days but fear I didn't fare so well.

I ran into my 1st Americans of the trip today. They passed me walking on the road into town. I knew they were Americans because they didn't say a word to me. Plus they were both wearing "flip flops". I want to start a society against men who wear "flip flops". Horrible. They annoyed me for the 5 minutes I heard that stupid slapping noise before they finally passed me. A bit later, at the computer place they rolled in. They reminded me of the boys from the plane: arrogant, affected. Kept talking loudly of how they were with a gang of boys "bumming around Europe on a boat." One got on a HAM radio to contact the aforementioned boat, for no particular reason. I couldn't place their accents, but they were trying to find flights back to the states. One was like "Hmm, London to NY, 300€, do you know anyone in NY?" and the other one was all "Yeah, I've got a place to bunk up in NY." "Bunk up." That got me. It sounded so American. So as I was getting up to go pay Tweedle Dee was saying to Tweedle Dum "How do you spell Siracusa?" "S-Y-R-A-C-U-S-A." So as I passed I smiled and said "It's S-I." "Oh!" "Well, guess we've got a seasoned traveller here." Such jerkstores, fuck you guys. I couldn't help correcting him, I just couldn't. Yeah, the American is "Syracuse" but TDee distinctly said "Siracus_a_". Heh. They either think I am a mysteriously smart and surprisingly non-French minx or I am a total bitch on wheels. I'm fine with either. Seeing them reminded me how much I prefer Italian boys. A good Italian boy is worth 20 of those stupid blockheads.

Germans beside me "Un grosse bierra!"

I want to respond to those questions you asked me about grand themes in terms of writing...my "sensibility". I gave that a lot of thought last year while I was here...it had never occurred to me to do that, and what you described to me as your perception of ~~ho~~ what my writing engenders (? right word?) ~~was~~ are all things that just seem to turn up. I wish I could consciously cultivate a sensibility, that's what I spent that time attempting to do last year. At the wedding a horrible American boy asked me the worst question ever "What do you write about?" My stock answer is "Many things, fools and kings" but I got paranoid about actually having no response. Should a writer be able to answer this? I tend to think the answer is obvious. Jane Austen said "love and money" because what else is there? That Foster Wallace guy said "I write about what it's like to be a fucking human being!"

In looking over things and looking ahead to an overarching theme that interests me I believe I was able to ~~commu~~ articulate was ~~the~~ miscommunications in the communication age. ~~Cr~~ Speechlessness or inability to articulate when more opportunities have

not saying
this right
how ironic

never been available. I'd like to write about the usuals that have no time and place but also give them ~~a~~ the backspin of this time and this place. I am terrible about talking about this stuff. I need to reread my little manifesto on the subject and then we should talk. But largely it's isolation in community, alone together, love without a net, false nets, where did my net go, who moved my net etc. Sometimes I think the net would be a parental model of a loving relationship, that gives a child the tools to love well. I go back and forth. All night on the ferry.

With anyone else I despise talking about writing but with you I think I just might enjoy it, and maybe even find it helpful. But generally I abhor talk about writing. Especially at weddings. "Do you think you have a book in you?" I could have kicked him!
"Yes, but I'm having an outpatient thing to take care of it."

      Outpatiently,
        Sensibility

May 1~~5~~6?/03

Dear B,

It's my last night in Lipari, some dubious
goaltending taking place behind me and
the tide is creeping ever-closer to my
knees. I've come to some sort of peace
about the letter thing, but we better not
talk about it, or I'm going to get all squir-
relly again. I see the German girls from
the boat tour yesterday. This really is a
small island. For some reason all the soccer ragazzi behind me are fat. What's up
with that? All of the things I want to tell
you in this letter I somehow feel I'd rather
tell you at a later date. The soccer ball
just rolled up to me and I rolled it back
and got the most charming smile from the
only thin kicker. Right before he takes a

shot he always makes this whistling noise. I love it. I could watch them all day. I just about did. So anyway, yeah. Ask me all about the volcano at night and Frau Sourpuss across from me on the boat. And Bartolo. Aieee. Whistle! (that was the kid.) He's even tricked out in a soccer jersey. I don't want to leave. Life is so much better here. Bartolo knows it. We were talking about NYC. He's been there. Said he liked it but he could never live there. Something about this place. Woops. I just let my cigarette burn down to my fingers while glazing over in an Italy-induced reverie. I'm packing up now. Hang on.

May 17. Hope you didn't hang on that whole time…I'm listening to the most annoying boy in the world for the blessedly last time. Oh! Just in time he found the squeak toy. I was afraid we were going to have to do without it. Thank God for small favours. I will not miss the constant aural chaos. But everything else: yes. This kid can't stop calling for his mama, it's the most irritating thing. I'd imitate it for you but there's a slight chance you wouldn't hear me. Either his mother constantly ignores him or she is dead. There's no way she can't hear, he's been doing it for over half an hour: "Maama!…Vieni!"…"MAA

MAA!" I hate to say it but ~~it make~~ my hatred of him is fuelled even further by the fact that he is fat. Overweight kids strike something foul into my heart. I don't like it about myself but there you go. I confess.

I talked to Lee on the phone today, incredibly—his mom finally gave it to him "Basta!" and now he is saying "Si! Si! Si! Si! Si! Si!" and I didn't think it could get more trying—he was still at work at 3:30 am. I needed to tell him he put the wrong version of my piece on the site. I think he changed it to the correct one. Oh my God I want to kill this kid. This is a crazy crazy family. Rosa and her wacky, afro-ed, overweight brood.

It's overcast today, somebody took mercy on me and made it a day it wouldn't be too painful to leave. Insolent child. Zito brutto bambino. I think I have a low tolerance for pointless brattiness because it was simply forbidden by my parents. You didn't even <u>think</u> of such behaviour. What was it like at your house? I have a feeling your parents gave you a bit of a longer leash. What with the no problems getting angry and yelling thing you've got going on. I just told the kid to shut up. It was either that or drop kick him into the marina. You would think someone running a villa would be more conscious of things that would disturb paying customers.

What a complaining letter. It's just cause I'm stuck here until I go to catch the boat. These are not ideal letter-writing conditions. La la la. Maybe I should shut myself in the bathroom and see if it's any quieter. Kids on the beach yesterday were torturing a jellyfish.

She charged me for laundry. I didn't ask them to do my laundry and I supplied my own detergent, but she charged me anyway. I hate shit like that. Hope I don't get seasick and toss my cookies tonight. Fabrizio made one last attempt at a date while I was in town. Fabrizio, what is he thinking? I saw mio capitano in the bookstore. I almost asked him for the other one's name. I liked him a lot. Maybe I will get the hell out of here and finish it on the pier. Post it before I go. I'm sorry your phone bill was so high. Mamma mia. It's the falling asleep on the phone that runs it up, though, caro. I blame the vodka for everything.

Hi again, well that plan didn't exactly work out, I had some running around to do and it looks like I'll send this tomorrow morning in Napoli...that's OK though, it just means you get to spend the night with me. On a boat! We haven't even left yet and already I feel like this is the greatest, most romantic thing in the world. My heart is filling up! I've never been on a boat this big! It's the greatest! I can run around exploring it. Hang out in a bar. Flirt with shipmen, go to the top deck and dream under the stars all night. Why have I never taken an overnight ferry before? And I dressed for voyaging: long black skirt with slit up front, pretty pink golf shirt (is that what they're called?) My cool new watch and bitchin' new ~~necklace~~ bracelet. ← I don't even have a necklace! I feel totally kitted out, as our limey friends would say. Plus I bought my monstrous bags of fruit. I only wish I had a great book to read. Décor in the reception lounge is cheesy turquoise 60's stewardess. I don't think it's possible for me to get seasick on a boat this size, but we'll see. I wonder what my cabin will look like, I'm waiting for Signor Reception. Oh B. This is the most fun. Big boat! Little me! In the morning: Napoli! Hey that rhymed. I think that calls for a song.

OK B, adorable S.R. just gave me my key

and I am lying on my bed. That was the best 22€ I've ever spent! This is so cool. I even have my own bathroom. It will be hard to get me out of this room, I fear. And so, are you awake yet? Yes, you must be, it's about 11 am, Americano. Turns out Lee will be in Maryland for a wedding next weekend so I may take the train there for a day. I couldn't find any fishing tackle that pleased me so that sucked. But il capitano was standing right beside me while I was leafing through something I got for you, so I know you'll treasure it always.

Italian sheets always look so spanking clean and glowing white, even in the shittiest dives where nothing works, the sheets will always look like they just came out of the store or off the loom or wherever sheets like this are made. I found some Aranciata senza zucchero. I keep trying to sleep away the bags under my eyes but it seems this time they are here for good. Every year I am able to get rid of them after about 2 weeks but no dice for la poverina in 2003. I guess this means I am officially old. One more thing we have in common.

Having a room alone also means the men don't get to bug you. Oh I love that. Did I ever tell you about how I fell in love at first sight on the train from Naples to Sorrento? It's true. I didn't think it was possible. Maybe I'll see him at the station. He wasn't supposed to get off before Sorrento but then he did and ruined everything. I wonder if I can sing in here without annoying anybody. There seem to be very few people in the cabins so I think I may go for it later.

C'mon, it's 5:25, let's haul anchor! I love fruit. I wanted one of everything. Or 5. One is fun—oh my! Major engine action starboard!—holy, OK I gotta go up on deck and say good-bye to Lipari...

Oh man.

I don't know why leaving things hurts me so much, but leaving a beautiful island on a large boat isn't doing myself any favours, and the three little boys who were standing way out on this little apse of land they would have had to court treachery and broken teeth to get onto, way out from the pier, who began waving and jumping up and down jubilantly the moment I opened the stairwell door onto the deck, despite the fact that the deck was crowded with people to wave to—

"Signorina! Signorina! Bella! Signorina! Bella!"—didn't help matters. It was like they were waiting for me. I felt very close to a sort of swoon, a collapse...little Italian boys get me. It felt big, the boat pulling away from a gorgeous, forgotten island and these kids calling out to me.

Maybe it was compounded by the fact that I saw my future pretty clearly yesterday afternoon. I'll tell you about it if you ask nicely. It's Italian faces, I love them so much it stirs something in my bones. When I see eyes or a demeanour or an expression like photos of my grandfather something primal comes over me. People are different here. Their faces are too.

I feel heartsick right now. Why did those boys have to be there on that crazy outcropping? Little crickets they looked like. The size of my thumbnail by the time I made it out to the deck. The island was gleaming and still, I saw everything. Then I went to the top deck and watched the other islands go by. This is definitely the highlight of my trip. It's breathtaking and wonderful how this gentle behemoth bears you through the ocean. How fun. I don't like the thought of leaving all the decent people I met there. I find it hard to see the good in people at home, but here they wear it to their teeth. If they're good, and most are, you see it. I'm tired of leaving them when it hurts me so much. I don't want to go back to my stupid life and my stupid job. None of my stupid friends will pick me up at the airport. So what if it's a holiday? Since when did they get lives? ¶ I think I'll go up top again—oh one funny thing, I saw a guy up there, ~~org~~ orange pants (?) and a "Roma, Candidate 2000" T-shirt. Leave it to an Italian to proudly don a short advertising the fact that Rome lost out to Beijing in the Olympic venue competition. So did Toronto and I'm glad. Stupid Toronto.

Ah, it's morning. I was awoken at some point by a German hippie who came to sleep in my cabin. It's 6:30 am and I see Napoli about 2 km away. How was your night? Oh wait, it's only midnight there. Maybe I should call. Oh but what with you keeping your cell phone off and everything, maybe not. I'm afraid I was grumpy with the German girl. She seemed very frightened of me this morning and was very sweet. That made me feel bad. She had a guitar and everything. Plus I got to see her in her underpants, which struck me as very German as well. OK, we're pulling in, I must go.

So Rome it is. I can't seem to get my letter-writing shit together with this one. It is as rainy and craptacular as ever in Napoli. I've always hated this city and the trend continues: the cab driver charged me 20€ for a 5 minute cab ride to the termini. With no shame he did that to me, it was the last dime I had. He made all these noises about how it was Sunday and he was even giving me a special price. They'll tell you you're beautiful and stick it to you anyway. Hate fucking Naples. That ride cost me more than the train ticket to Rome. Very overcast. I imagine this is what I can look forward to at home. Look at me again, all sour. I'm very tired. And out of fruit.

Oh, but let me tell you one thing, about telling me things: I am not a Flaubert-forgetter. If you had received my letters (as you can see, this will be a theme) you would have gotten the passage from "Earthly Powers" which was a kind of response to Flaubert (all my books started talking to one another). The narrator, a writer, talked about how it was folly to think there was anything more important than clichés and writers make themselves most ridiculous when trying to pretend there isn't. He is an 81 year old, looking back at life. I raved and raved about this book, I loved it. So there's no shame in cliché, and people will never get tired of reading them. Or hearing them. So fuck Flaubert.

There were several things from that book I had to write out for you. I loved AB's style so much. It had class. And that British decorum in talking about less-than-decorous things. I ♥ that. Ah, cattle galloping through field. Where do you think you're going? "Race you to the fence!"

I didn't see my one and only in the termini. I didn't see much of anything I was so crushed/furious about that cab driver. So these movies you talk about...which will we see? Not X-Men or Matrix, as I have not seen the first of either. I guess it will be exciting to have some movies waiting for me. Can't believe I'll be home tomorrow. I like listening to the people beside me. Strangers who haven't stopped talking since they sat down. I can't quite figure out if they are flirting. Oh I see now they are. It's all in the body language. They look like lonely, lovely people. I'm glad I stole that girl's seat so that she was forced to sit across from her future husband/object of derision. I bought a barfy British ladies' magazine for mindless diversion. How can I resist with a story that advertises "How to be lucky in love, life, <u>everything</u>!" They have formulas and checklists! This is it, B! The answers have finally found me! By the time I get to Rome I should be the luckiest son of a bitch in the Republic.

                        Good-bye to all that,

                                          Michelle

Michelle Orange lives in New York City.